SLOW STOPPERS

The expression Good Housekeeping as used
title of the book is the trademark of The National
Magazine Company and The Hearst Corporation,
registered in the United Kingdom and USA, and
other principal countries of the world, and is the
absolute property of The National Magazine
Company and The Hearst Corporation. The use
of this trademark other than with the express
permission of The National Magazine Company
or The Hearst Corporation is strictly prohibited.

The Good Housekeeping website is
www.goodhousekeeping.co.uk

ISBN 978-1-909397-05-7

A catalogue record for this book is available from
the British Library.

Reproduction by Dot Gradations Ltd, UK
Printed and bound by
1010 Printing International Ltd, China

This book can be ordered direct from the publisher.
Contact the marketing department, but try your
bookshop first.

www.anovabooks.com

NOTES
Both metric and imperial measures are given for
the recipes. Follow either set of measures, not a
mixture of both, as they are not interchangeable.

All spoon measures are level.
1 tsp = 5ml spoon; 1 tbsp = 15ml spoon.

Ovens and grills must be preheated to the specified
temperature.

Medium eggs should be used except where
otherwise specified. Free-range eggs are
recommended.

Note that some recipes contain raw or lightly
cooked eggs. The young, elderly, pregnant women
and anyone with an immune-deficiency disease
should avoid these because of the slight risk of
salmonella.

Contents

Slow-cooker
Starters and Sides

Carrot and Coriander Soup

Slow Cooker Recipe

Hands-on time: 15 minutes
Cooking time: 15 minutes in pan, then about 4 hours on High, plus cooling

40g (1½oz) butter
175g (6oz) leeks, trimmed and sliced
450g (1lb) carrots, sliced
2 tsp ground coriander
1 tsp plain flour
1 litre (1¾ pints) hot vegetable stock
  (see page 44)
150ml (¼ pint) single cream
salt and freshly ground black pepper
fresh coriander leaves, roughly torn,
  to serve

WITHOUT A SLOW COOKER

Complete steps 1 and 2. In step 3, bring to the boil and leave the soup in the pan. Season with salt and ground black pepper, then reduce the heat, cover the pan and simmer for about 20 minutes until the vegetables are tender. Complete step 4 to finish the recipe.

1 Melt the butter in a large pan. Stir in the leeks and carrots, then cover the pan and cook gently for 7–10 minutes until the vegetables begin to soften but not colour.

2 Stir in the ground coriander and flour and cook, stirring, for 1 minute.

3 Add the hot stock and bring to the boil, stirring. Season with salt and ground black pepper, then transfer to the slow cooker, cover and cook on High for 3–4 hours until the vegetables are tender.

4 Leave the soup to cool a little, then whiz in batches in a blender or food processor until smooth. Pour into a clean pan and stir in the cream. Adjust the seasoning and reheat gently on the hob – do not boil. Ladle into warmed bowls, scatter with torn coriander leaves and serve.

Serves 6

Beetroot Soup

Hands-on time: 15 minutes
Cooking time: 15 minutes in pan, then about 4 hours on High

1 tbsp olive oil

1 onion, finely chopped

750g (1lb 11oz) raw beetroot, peeled and cut into 1cm (½in) cubes

275g (10oz) potatoes, roughly chopped

1.5 litres (2½ pints) hot vegetable stock (see page 44)

juice of 1 lemon

salt and freshly ground black pepper

To serve

125ml (4fl oz) soured cream

25g (1oz) mixed root vegetable crisps (optional)

2 tbsp snipped fresh chives

1. Heat the oil in a large pan. Add the onion and cook for 5 minutes to soften. Add the beetroot and potatoes and cook for a further 5 minutes.

2. Add the hot stock and the lemon juice and bring to the boil. Season with salt and ground black pepper, then transfer to the slow cooker, cover and cook on High for 3–4 hours until the beetroot is tender.

3. Leave the soup to cool a little, then whiz in batches in a blender or food processor until smooth. Pour into a clean pan and reheat gently on the hob – do not boil. Ladle into warmed bowls. Swirl 1 tbsp soured cream on each portion, scatter with a few vegetable crisps, if you like, and sprinkle with snipped chives to serve.

Complete step 1. In step 2, bring to the boil and leave the soup in the pan, then reduce the heat and simmer gently, half-covered, for 25 minutes. Complete the recipe to serve.

FREEZE AHEAD

To make ahead and freeze, prepare the soup to the end of step 2, then cool half or all the soup, pack and freeze for up to three months. To use, thaw the soup overnight and simmer over a low heat for 5 minutes.

Serves 8

French Onion Soup

Hands-on time: 30 minutes
Cooking time: 40 minutes in pan, then about 4 hours on Low

75g (3oz) butter

700g (1½lb) onions, sliced

3 garlic cloves, crushed

1 tbsp plain flour

200ml (7fl oz) dry white wine

1 litre (1¾ pints) hot vegetable stock
(see page 44)

bouquet garni (1 bay leaf, a few fresh
thyme and parsley sprigs)

salt and freshly ground black pepper

To serve

1 small baguette, cut into slices 1cm
(½in) thick

50g (2oz) Gruyère cheese or
Cheddar, grated

WITHOUT A SLOW COOKER

Complete step 1. In step 2, bring to
the boil, then reduce the heat and
simmer gently, uncovered, for 20–30
minutes. Complete steps 3 and 4 to
finish the recipe.

1. Melt the butter in a large pan. Add the onions and cook slowly over a very low heat, stirring frequently, until very soft and golden brown – this should take at least 30 minutes. Add the garlic and flour and cook, stirring, for 1 minute.

2. Pour in the wine and let bubble until reduced by half. Add the hot stock, the bouquet garni and seasoning and bring to the boil. Transfer to the slow cooker, cover and cook on Low for 3–4 hours until the onions are meltingly tender.

3. When ready to serve, preheat the grill. Lightly toast the slices of baguette on both sides. Reheat the soup and adjust the seasoning. Discard the bouquet garni.

4. Divide the soup among four ovenproof soup bowls. Float two or three slices of toast on each portion and sprinkle thickly with the grated cheese. Stand the bowls under the hot grill until the cheese has melted and turned golden brown. Serve at once.

Serves 4

Leek and Potato Soup

Slow Cooker Recipe

🍴 **Hands-on time:** 10 minutes
Cooking time: 30 minutes in pan, then about 4 hours on Low, plus cooling

25g (1oz) butter

1 onion, finely chopped

1 garlic clove, crushed

550g (1¼lb) leeks, trimmed and chopped

200g (7oz) floury potatoes, sliced

1.1 litres (2 pints) hot vegetable stock (see page 44)

crème fraîche and chopped chives to garnish

WITHOUT A SLOW COOKER

Complete step 1. In step 2, bring to the boil, then reduce the heat and simmer for 20 minutes until the potatoes are tender. Complete steps 3 and 4 to finish the recipe.

1 Melt the butter in a pan over a gentle heat. Add the onion and cook for 10–15 minutes until soft. Add the garlic and cook for a further 1 minute. Add the leeks and cook for 5–10 minutes until softened. Add the potatoes and toss together with the leeks.

2 Pour in the hot stock and bring to the boil. Transfer the soup to the slow cooker, cover and cook on Low for 3–4 hours until the potatoes are tender.

3 Leave the soup to cool a little, then whiz in batches in a blender or food processor until smooth.

4 Pour the soup into a clean pan and reheat gently on the hob – do not boil. Ladle into warmed bowls, garnish with crème fraîche and chives and serve.

Serves 4

Split Pea and Ham Soup

Hands-on time: 15 minutes, plus overnight soaking
Cooking time: 20 minutes in pan, then about 4 hours on High, plus cooling

500g pack of dried yellow split peas, soaked overnight (see Save Money, opposite)

25g (1oz) butter

1 large onion, finely chopped

125g (4oz) rindless smoked streaky bacon rashers, roughly chopped

1 garlic clove, crushed

1.7 litres (3 pints) well-flavoured ham or vegetable stock

1 bouquet garni (1 bay leaf, a few fresh parsley and thyme sprigs)

1 tsp dried oregano

125g (4oz) chopped cooked ham

salt and freshly ground black pepper

cracked black pepper to serve

1 Drain the soaked split peas. Melt the butter in a large pan, add the onion, bacon and garlic and cook over a low heat for about 10 minutes until the onion is soft.

2 Add the split peas to the pan with the stock. Bring to the boil and use a slotted spoon to remove any scum that comes to the surface. Add the bouquet garni and oregano, then season with salt and ground black pepper. Transfer to the slow cooker, cover and cook on High for 3–4 hours until the peas are very soft.

3 Leave the soup to cool a little, then whiz half the soup in a blender or food processor until smooth. Pour all the soup into a clean pan and reheat gently on the hob – do not boil. Add the ham and check the seasoning. Ladle into warmed bowls and sprinkle with cracked black pepper to serve.

Dried peas form the base of this comforting soup and are much cheaper than canned peas. First, you need to soak them overnight in about 1 litre (1¾ pints) cold water. If you forget, put them straight into a pan with the water, bring to the boil and cook for 1–2 minutes, then leave to stand for 2 hours before using.

Serves 6

Perfect Veg

Nutritious, mouth-watering and essential to a healthy diet – vegetables are ideal for adding to slow-cooked dishes.

Stewing

1 Cut the vegetables into large bite-size pieces, no more than about 5cm (2in) square. Put them into a heatproof casserole (for oven cooking) or a heavy-based pan (for hob cooking). Add salt and freshly ground black pepper and flavourings, if you like (see Perfect stews opposite), and mix well.

2 Preheat the oven to 180°C (160°C fan oven) mark 4 if you are cooking in the oven.

3 Pour in enough hot stock to come about three-quarters of the way up the vegetables. Cover the dish with a lid or foil and cook for 30–40 minutes until the vegetables are tender but not disintegrating. Turn the vegetables once during cooking and baste with the juices a few times.

Perfect stews

- ❏ Any vegetable can be stewed; be careful not to overcook it
- ❏ Ideal flavourings for stewed vegetables include garlic, shallots, curry powder (or Indian spices), and chilli sauce or chopped chilli
- ❏ Potatoes will thicken the dish a little as they release some of their starch

Perfect braising

- ❏ Carrots, fennel, leeks, celeriac, celery and cabbage are all good braised
- ❏ Leave vegetables whole or cut them into chunks. Shred cabbage, then fry lightly before braising
- ❏ Cook the vegetables in a single layer

Braising

1 Prepare the vegetables (see Perfect braising above). Pack tightly in a single layer in an ovenproof dish. Preheat the oven to 180°C (160°C fan oven) mark 4. Dot the vegetables generously with butter and season with salt.

2 Pour in enough hot stock to come halfway up the vegetables. Cover the dish with a lid or foil and cook for 30-40 minutes until the vegetables are soft. Baste them with the buttery stock a few times during cooking.

Braised Chicory in White Wine

Slow Cooker Recipe

Hands-on time: 5 minutes
Cooking time: about 3 hours on Low

50g (2oz) butter, softened
6 chicory heads, trimmed
juice of ½ lemon
100ml (3½fl oz) white wine
salt and freshly ground black pepper
snipped fresh chives to serve

1 Grease the slow cooker dish with 15g (½oz) of the butter. Toss the chicory in the lemon juice and arrange in the bottom of the dish.

2 Season to taste, add the wine and dot the remaining butter over the top. Cover and cook on Low for 2–3 hours until soft. Scatter with chives to serve.

WITHOUT A SLOW COOKER

Grease a 1.7 litre (3 pint) ovenproof dish instead of the slow cooker. Complete step 1 and the first part of step 2. Cover with foil and cook in the oven for 1 hour until soft. Scatter with chives to serve.

Serves 4

Braised Red Cabbage

Slow Cooker Recipe

Hands-on time: 10 minutes
Cooking time: about 3 hours on Low

1 red onion, finely chopped

½ medium red cabbage (weight about 500g/1lb 2oz), shredded

1 Bramley apple, peeled, cored and chopped

25g (1oz) light muscovado sugar

1 cinnamon stick

a pinch of ground cloves

¼ tsp freshly grated nutmeg

2 tbsp each red wine vinegar and red wine

juice of 1 orange

salt and freshly ground black pepper

1 Put all the ingredients into the slow cooker and stir to mix well. Cover and cook on Low for 2–3 hours.

2 When the cabbage is tender, take the pan off the heat and discard the cinnamon stick. Serve at once, or leave to cool, then put into a bowl, cover and chill the cabbage overnight.

WITHOUT A SLOW COOKER

Heat 2 tbsp olive oil in a large heavy-based pan. Add the onion and cook gently for 3–4 minutes to soften. Add the cabbage, sugar, spices, vinegars and orange juice and season well. Bring to the boil, then reduce the heat, cover the pan and simmer for 30 minutes. Add the apples and stir through. Cook for a further 15 minutes or until the cabbage is tender and nearly all the liquid has evaporated. Discard the cinnamon stick before serving.

3 To reheat, put the cabbage into a pan, add 2 tbsp cold water and cover with a tight-fitting lid. Bring to the boil, then reduce the heat and simmer for 25 minutes.

Serves 8

Ratatouille

Slow Cooker Recipe

Hands-on time: 20 minutes
Cooking time: 15 minutes in pan, then about 4 hours on High

4 tbsp olive oil

2 onions, thinly sliced

1 large garlic clove, crushed

350g (12oz) small aubergines,
    thinly sliced

450g (1lb) small courgettes, thinly sliced

450g (1lb) tomatoes, skinned, seeded
    and roughly chopped

1 green and 1 red pepper, each seeded
    and sliced

1 tbsp freshly chopped basil

2 tsp freshly chopped thyme

2 tbsp freshly chopped flat-leafed parsley

2 tbsp sun-dried tomato paste

salt and freshly ground black pepper

1 Heat the oil in a large pan. Add the onions and garlic and fry gently for 10 minutes or until softened and golden.

2 Add the aubergines, courgettes, tomatoes, sliced peppers, herbs, tomato paste and seasoning and fry, stirring, for 2–3 minutes.

3 Transfer to the slow cooker, cover and cook on High for 3–4 hours until all the vegetables are tender. Taste and adjust the seasoning. Serve the ratatouille hot or at room temperature

WITHOUT A SLOW COOKER

Complete steps 1 and 2. In step 3, leave the mixture in the pan, cover tightly and simmer for 30 minutes or until all the vegetables are tender. Uncover towards the end if there is too much liquid. Season and serve as described in step 3.

Serves 6

Mushroom and Bean Hotpot

Slow Cooker Recipe

Hands-on time: 15 minutes
Cooking time: 15 minutes in pan, then about 3 hours on Low

3 tbsp olive oil

700g (1½lb) chestnut mushrooms, roughly chopped

1 large onion, finely chopped

2 tbsp plain flour

2 tbsp mild curry paste

150ml (¼ pint) dry white wine

400g can chopped tomatoes

2 tbsp sun-dried tomato paste

2 × 400g cans mixed beans, drained and rinsed

3 tbsp mango chutney

3 tbsp freshly chopped coriander and mint

1 Heat the oil in a large pan over a low heat. Add the mushrooms and onion and fry until the onion is soft and dark golden. Stir in the flour and curry paste and cook for 1–2 minutes, then add the wine, tomatoes, tomato paste and beans.

2 Bring to the boil, then transfer to the slow cooker, cover and cook on Low for 2–3 hours.

3 Stir in the mango chutney and chopped herbs and serve.

WITHOUT A SLOW COOKER

Complete step 1. In step 2, leave the mixture in the pan and bring to the boil, then reduce the heat and simmer for 30 minutes or until most of the liquid has reduced. Complete step 3 to finish the recipe.

Serves 6

Lentils with Red Pepper

Hands-on time: 10 minutes
Cooking time: 20 minutes in pan, then about 4 hours on High

1 tbsp olive oil

1 large onion, finely chopped

2 celery sticks, diced

2 carrots, diced

2 bay leaves, torn

300g (11oz) Puy lentils

600ml (1 pint) hot vegetable stock
(see page 44)

1 marinated red pepper, drained
and chopped

2 tbsp freshly chopped flat-leafed
parsley, plus extra to garnish

freshly ground black pepper

1 Heat the oil in a pan. Add the onion
and cook over a low heat for 15
minutes or until soft. Add the celery,
carrots and bay leaves and cook for
2 minutes.

2 Add the lentils with the hot stock and
stir everything together. Transfer to
the slow cooker, cover and cook on
High for 3–4 hours.

3 Stir in the red pepper and parsley and
season with ground black pepper.
Leave to stand for 10 minutes, then
garnish with extra parsley and serve
as an accompaniment.

WITHOUT A SLOW COOKER

Complete step 1. In step 2, leave the
mixture in the pan, half cover with
a lid and simmer over a low heat for
25–30 minutes. Complete step 3 to
finish the recipe.

Serves 4

Spiced Bean and Vegetable Stew

Hands-on time: 15 minutes
Cooking time: 10 minutes in pan, then about 3 hours on Low

Slow Cooker Recipe

3 tbsp olive oil

2 small onions, sliced

2 garlic cloves, crushed

1 tbsp sweet paprika

1 small dried red chilli, seeded and finely chopped

700g (1½lb) sweet potatoes, cubed

700g (1½lb) pumpkin, cut into chunks

125g (4oz) okra, trimmed

500g jar passata

400g can haricot or cannellini beans, drained and rinsed

450ml (¾ pint) hot vegetable stock (see page 44)

salt and freshly ground black pepper

1 Heat the oil in a large pan over a very gentle heat. Add the onions and garlic and cook for 5 minutes.

2 Stir in the paprika and chilli and cook for 2 minutes, then add the sweet potatoes, pumpkin, okra, passata, beans and hot stock. Season generously with salt and ground black pepper and bring to the boil.

3 Transfer to the slow cooker, cover and cook on Low for 2–3 hours until the vegetables are tender.

SAVE EFFORT

An easy way to get a differently flavoured dish is to use 1 tsp each ground cumin and ground coriander instead of paprika. Garnish the stew with freshly chopped coriander.

WITHOUT A SLOW COOKER

Complete the recipe to the end of step 2, but leaving out the beans. Cover the pan and simmer for 20 minutes or until the vegetables are tender. Add the beans and cook for 3 minutes to warm through. Serve immediately.

Serves 6

Poultry and Game Dishes

Perfect Poultry

Poultry and game birds are available all year round to feast on, but as a lot of game birds are unfarmed, there are seasonal fluctuations. Where possible, when you are buying poultry and game birds, try to support your local butcher. You will be rewarded with great produce and choice.

Hygiene

- ❑ Raw poultry and meat contain harmful bacteria that can spread easily to anything they touch
- ❑ Always wash your hands, kitchen surfaces, chopping boards, knives and equipment before and after handling poultry or meat
- ❑ Don't let raw poultry or meat touch other foods
- ❑ Always cover raw poultry and meat and store in the bottom of the fridge, where they can't touch or drip on to other foods

Poultry comparison chart

1 Duck
2 Guinea fowl
3 Chicken
4 Poussin
5 Pheasant

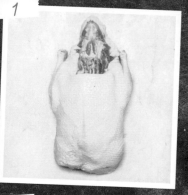

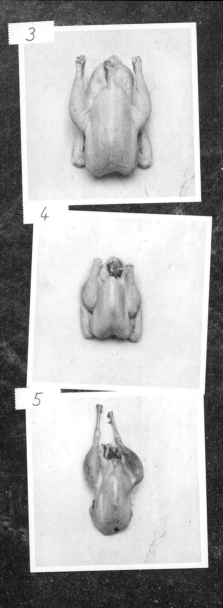

3

4

5

Types of chicken

Corn-fed These chickens are fed on corn rather than standard chicken feed and have golden yellow flesh and, often, an improved flavour. They weigh about 2kg (4½lb).

Roasting Usually young birds, chickens for roasting are tender and weigh about 2kg (4½lb).

Boiling These birds are usually about 18 months old and have tougher flesh that is better suited to long, slow cooking such as stewing, poaching, casseroling or pot-roasting. They usually weigh around 2.5–3kg (5½–6½lb).

Poussins Usually four to eight weeks old, they weigh only about 450g (1lb). Whole poussin can be roasted or spatchcocked and grilled; portions can be pan-fried, grilled, braised and pot-roasted.

How to Joint a Chicken

You can buy pieces of chicken in a supermarket or from a butcher, but it is more economical to joint a whole bird yourself. Use the wing tips and bones to make stock (see page 44).

1   Using a sharp meat knife with a curved blade, cut out the wishbone (see page 60) and remove the wings in a single piece. Remove the wing tips.

2   With the tail pointing towards you and breast side up, pull one leg away from the body and cut through the skin between the leg and breast. Pull the leg down until you crack the joint between the thigh bone and ribcage. Cut through that joint, then cut through the remaining leg meat. Repeat on the other side.

3   To remove the breast without any bone, make a cut along the length of the breastbone. Gently teasing the flesh away from the ribs with the knife, work the blade down between the flesh and ribs of one breast and cut it off neatly. (Always cut in, towards the bone.) Repeat on the other side.

4   To remove the breast with the bone in, make a cut along the full length of the breastbone. Using poultry shears, cut through the breastbone, then cut through the ribcage following the outline of the breast meat. Repeat on the other side. Trim off any flaps of skin or fat.

3

Perfect Casseroling

There are a number of ways to make the most of the delicate taste of poultry. Here's how to make the perfect casserole.

Chicken casserole

To serve 4–6, you will need:
1 jointed chicken, 3 tbsp oil,
1 chopped onion, 2 crushed garlic cloves, 2 chopped celery sticks,
2 chopped carrots, 1 tbsp plain flour,
2 tbsp freshly chopped tarragon or thyme, chicken stock and/or wine,
salt and freshly ground black pepper

1 Preheat the oven to 180°C (160°C fan oven) mark 4. Cut the chicken legs and breasts in half.

2 Heat the oil in a flameproof casserole and brown the chicken all over. Remove the chicken and pour off the excess oil. Add the onion and garlic and brown for a few minutes. Add the vegetables, then stir in the flour and cook for 1 minute. Add the herbs and season. Add the chicken and pour in the stock and/or wine to come three-quarters of the way up the poultry. Bring to the boil, then cover and cook in the oven for 1–1½ hours.

Slow-braised Garlic Chicken

Hands-on time: 30 minutes, plus cooling
Cooking time: about 2 hours

2 tbsp olive oil

1 tbsp freshly chopped thyme

125g (4oz) chestnut mushrooms, finely chopped

6 whole chicken legs (drumsticks and thighs)

18 thin slices pancetta

2 tbsp plain flour

25g (1oz) butter

18 small shallots

12 garlic cloves, unpeeled but split

750ml bottle full-bodied white wine, such as Chardonnay

2 bay leaves

salt and freshly ground black pepper

1 Preheat the oven to 180°C (160°C fan oven) mark 4. Heat 1 tbsp of the oil in a frying pan. Add the thyme and mushrooms and fry until the moisture has evaporated. Season with salt and ground black pepper and leave to cool.

2 Loosen the skin away from one chicken leg and spoon a little of the mushroom paste underneath. Season the leg all over with salt and pepper, then wrap three pancetta slices around the thigh end. Repeat with the remaining chicken legs, then dust using 1 tbsp of the flour.

3 Melt the butter in a frying pan with the remaining oil over a high heat. Fry the chicken legs, in batches, seam side down, until golden. Turn the legs and brown the other side – the browning should take 8–10 minutes per batch, then transfer to a casserole.

4 Put the shallots and garlic into the frying pan and cook for 10 minutes or until browned. Sprinkle with the remaining flour and cook for 1 minute. Pour in the wine and bring to the boil, stirring. Pour into the casserole with the chicken and add the bay leaves. Cover and cook in the oven for 1½ hours. Serve hot.

FREEZE AHEAD

To make ahead and freeze, complete the recipe. Cool quickly, then freeze in an airtight container for up to one month. To use, thaw overnight at cool room temperature. Preheat the oven to 220°C (200°C fan oven) mark 7. Put the chicken back into the casserole and reheat in the oven for 15 minutes. Reduce the oven temperature to 180°C (160°C fan oven) mark 4 and cook for a further 25 minutes.

Serves 6

Classic Coq au Vin

Hands-on time: 15 minutes
Cooking time: about 2¼ hours

1 large chicken, jointed (see page 36), or 6–8 chicken joints

2 tbsp well-seasoned flour

100g (3½oz) butter

125g (4oz) lean bacon, diced

1 medium onion, quartered

1 medium carrot, quartered

4 tbsp brandy

600ml (1 pint) red wine

1 garlic clove, crushed

1 bouquet garni (2 bay leaves, a few fresh parsley and thyme sprigs)

1 tsp sugar

2 tbsp vegetable oil

450g (1lb) button onions

a pinch of sugar

1 tsp wine vinegar

225g (8oz) button mushrooms

6 slices white bread, crusts removed

salt and freshly ground black pepper

1 Coat the chicken pieces with 1 tbsp of the seasoned flour. Melt 25g (1oz) of the butter in a flameproof casserole. Add the chicken and fry until golden brown on all sides. Add the bacon, onion quarters and carrot and fry until softened.

2 Heat the brandy in a small pan, pour over the chicken and ignite, shaking the pan. Pour in the wine and stir to dislodge any sediment from the bottom of the casserole. Add the garlic, bouquet garni and sugar cube and bring to the boil. Reduce the heat, cover and simmer for 1–1½ hours until the chicken is cooked through.

3 Meanwhile, melt 25g (1oz) of the butter with 1 tsp of the oil in a frying pan. Add the button onions and fry until they begin to brown. Add the sugar and vinegar together with 1 tbsp water. Cover and simmer for 10–15 minutes until just tender. Keep warm.

4 Melt 25g (1oz) of the butter with 2 tsp of the oil in a pan. Add the mushrooms and cook for a few minutes, then turn off the heat and keep warm. Remove the chicken from the casserole and place in a

dish. Surround with the onions and mushrooms and keep hot.

5 Discard the bouquet garni. Skim the excess fat from the cooking liquid, then boil for 3–5 minutes until reduced. Add the remaining oil to the fat in the frying pan and fry the bread until golden brown on both sides. Cut each slice into triangles.

6 Work the remaining butter and flour together to make a beurre manié. Take the casserole off the heat and add small pieces of the beurre manié to the liquid. Stir until smooth, then put back on the hob and bring just to the boil. The sauce should be thick and shiny. Take off the heat and season. Put the chicken, onions and mushrooms back into the casserole and stir. Serve with the fried bread.

Serves 6

Stoved Chicken

Hands-on time: 15 minutes
Cooking time: about 2½ hours

25g (1oz) butter, plus a little extra

1 tbsp vegetable oil

4 chicken quarters, halved

125g (4oz) lean back bacon, rind removed and chopped

1.1kg (2½lb) floury potatoes, such as King Edward, cut into 5mm (¼in) slices

2 large onions, sliced

2 tsp freshly chopped thyme or ½ tsp dried thyme

600ml (1 pint) hot chicken stock (see page 44)

salt and freshly ground black pepper

snipped fresh chives to garnish

1 Preheat the oven to 150°C (130°C fan oven) mark 2. Heat half the butter and the oil in a large frying pan and fry the chicken and bacon for 5 minutes or until lightly browned.

2 Layer half the potato slices, then half the onion slices in the bottom of a large casserole. Season well, add the thyme and dot with half the remaining butter.

3 Add the chicken and bacon, season to taste and dot with the remaining butter. Cover with the remaining onions and finally a layer of potatoes. Season and dot with a little more butter. Pour the hot stock over.

4 Cover and cook in the oven for about 2½ hours until the chicken is tender and the potatoes are cooked, adding a little more hot stock if necessary.

5 Just before serving, sprinkle with snipped chives.

3 Good Stocks

Vegetable Stock

To make 1.1 litres (2 pints), you will need:

225g (8oz) roughly chopped onions, 225g (8oz) roughly chopped celery sticks, 225g (8oz) trimmed and roughly chopped leeks, 225g (8oz) roughly chopped carrots, 2 bay leaves, a few fresh thyme sprigs, 1 small bunch of parsley, 10 black peppercorns, ½ tsp sea salt.

1 Put the onions, celery, leeks and carrots into a large pan. Add 1.7 litres (3 pints) cold water, the bay leaves, thyme sprigs, parsley, peppercorns and salt, then bring slowly to the boil and skim the surface.

2 Partially cover the pan, then reduce the heat and simmer for 30 minutes; check the seasoning. Strain the stock through a fine sieve into a bowl and leave to cool. Cover and keep in the fridge for up to three days. Use as required.

Chicken Stock

To make 1.1 litres (2 pints), you will need:

225g (8oz) roughly chopped onions, 150g (5oz) trimmed and roughly chopped leeks, 225g (8oz) roughly chopped celery sticks, 1.6kg (3½lb) raw chicken bones, 1 bouquet garni (2 bay leaves, a few fresh parsley and thyme sprigs), 1 tsp black peppercorns, ½ tsp sea salt.

1 Put all the ingredients into a large pan and pour in 3 litres (5¼ pints) cold water. Bring slowly to the boil and skim the surface.

2 Partially cover the pan, reduce the heat and simmer gently for 2 hours; check the seasoning.

3 Strain the stock through a fine sieve into a bowl and cool quickly. Cover and keep in the fridge for up to three days. Remove the solidified fat from the surface and use the stock as required.

Giblet Stock

To make 1.3 litres (2¼ pints), you
will need:
turkey giblets, 1 quartered onion,
1 halved carrot, 1 halved celery stick,
6 black peppercorns, 1 bay leaf.

1 Put the giblets into a large pan,
   add the onion, carrot, celery,
   peppercorns and bay leaf and
   pour in 1.5 litres (2½ pints) cold
   water. Cover and bring to the boil.
2 Reduce the heat and simmer for
   30 minutes–1 hour, skimming
   occasionally. Strain through a
   sieve. Cool quickly, put into a
   sealable container and chill for
   up to three days.

Chicken and Pork Terrine

🍴 **Hands-on time:** 30 minutes, plus overnight chilling
Cooking time: about 2 hours 10 minutes, plus cooling

1 tbsp olive oil, plus extra to brush

1 onion, finely chopped

2 tbsp brandy (optional)

12 smoked streaky bacon rashers

2 skinless chicken breasts, cut into
1cm (½in) pieces (or use turkey breast
or mince)

500g pack of pork mince

50g (2oz) pistachios, roughly chopped

50g (2oz) dried cranberries

¾ tsp freshly grated nutmeg

2 fresh thyme sprigs, leaves picked off

salt and freshly ground black pepper

fruit chutney and toast to serve

1 Heat the oil in a medium pan and cook
   the onion gently for 10 minutes or until
   softened. Carefully add the brandy,
   if you like, and bubble for 30 seconds,
   then tip the mixture into a large bowl
   and leave to cool.

2 Preheat the oven to 180°C (160°C
   fan oven) mark 4. Use about 10 of
   the bacon rashers to line the inside
   of a 900g (2lb) loaf tin, leaving the

excess hanging over the sides. Add
the chopped chicken, pork, pistachios,
cranberries, nutmeg, thyme leaves
and plenty of seasoning (it needs a fair
amount of salt) to the cooled onion
mixture and mix well.

3 Press the mixture into the prepared
   loaf tin and level the surface. Fold any
   overhanging bacon over the filling and
   cover with the remaining rashers. Press
   down again to make sure the surface is
   smooth. Lightly oil a small sheet of foil
   and press on top of the loaf tin. Wrap
   the tin well in a further double layer of
   foil, then put into a roasting tin. Half-fill
   the roasting tin with boiling water
   from the kettle and carefully transfer
   to the oven.

4 Cook for 1½ hours or until the terrine
   feels solid when pressed. Lift the tin out
   of the water. Unwrap the outer layers
   of foil (leaving the greased foil layer
   in place). Carefully pour out any liquid
   from the terrine (this will set into a jelly
   if not done). Leave to cool.

5 Sit the loaf tin on a baking tray and place three cans of tomatoes (or similar) on top of the terrine (resting on the foil layer). Chill overnight.

6 When ready to serve, preheat the oven to 200°C (180°C fan oven) mark 6. Unmould the terrine on to a baking tray and lightly brush with oil. Brown in the oven for 20–25 minutes (if you don't want the terrine browned, leave this step out). Serve the terrine warm or at room temperature in slices, with fruit chutney and toast.

SAVE TIME

Prepare the terrine to the end of step 5 up to two days ahead. Remove the weights and chill again. Complete the recipe to serve.

Serves 8

Perfect Turkey

Cooking a turkey can be a daunting prospect, especially since quite often it is a once-a-year meal. However, with planning and by following a few simple steps, you can produce a perfectly cooked turkey for any occasion.

Thawing

Leave a frozen turkey in its bag and thaw at cool room temperature, not in the fridge. Remove any giblets as soon as they become loose. Once there are no ice crystals inside the body cavity and the legs are flexible, cover the turkey and store in the fridge. Cook within 24 hours.

Cleaning the bird

Before stuffing a bird, pull out and discard any loose fat from the neck or cavity with your fingers. Then dry the bird well using kitchen paper.

Preparing the bird

Take the bird out of the fridge 45 minutes–1 hour before stuffing and roasting to allow it to reach room temperature, then clean it (see right).

Stuffing

Loosely stuff the neck end only. Allow 225g (8oz) stuffing for each 2.3kg (5lb) weight of bird and stuff just before cooking. Secure the neck skin with skewers or cocktail sticks, or sew using a trussing needle threaded with fine string.

Resting

Once the bird is cooked, allow the turkey to rest for 20-30 minutes before carving. Transfer from the roasting tin to a plate, cover loosely with foil and a clean teatowel. Resting allows the juices to settle back into the meat, leaving it moist and easier to carve.

Cooking

Weigh the bird after stuffing to calculate the cooking time. Coat the turkey with butter and season. Wrap loosely in a 'tent' of foil, then cook in an oven preheated to 190°C (170°C fan oven) mark 5. Allow 45 minutes per 1kg (2¼lb) (20 minutes per 450g (1lb), plus 20 minutes (see chart on page 62 for timings). Remove the foil about 1 hour before the end of cooking time to brown the bird. Baste regularly. Test that the turkey is cooked (see page 63) and if not, cook a little longer.

Clementine and Sage Turkey with Madeira Gravy

Hands-on time: 30 minutes
Cooking time: about 3 hours 40 minutes, plus resting

5.4kg (12lb) free-range turkey (keep the giblets for stock, if you like to one side – see page 44. Spend as much as you can on your turkey – you'll notice the difference in the texture and taste)

3 firm clementines

20g pack of fresh sage

100g (3½oz) butter, softened

500g (1lb 2oz) stuffing (see pages 56–9)

3 celery sticks

3 carrots, halved lengthways

salt and freshly ground black pepper

fried clementine halves and stuffing balls to garnish (optional)

For the Madeira gravy

25g (1oz) plain flour

125ml (4fl oz) Madeira wine

300ml (½ pint) chicken stock (see page 44)

1 tbsp runny honey or redcurrant jelly, if needed

1 Remove the turkey from the fridge 1 hour before you stuff it to let it come up to room temperature.

2 Preheat the oven to 190°C (170°C fan oven) mark 5. Finely grate the zest from the clementines into a medium bowl. Halve the zest-free clementines and put to one side. Next, add 2 tbsp thinly sliced sage leaves (keep the rest of the bunch to one side) to the bowl with the butter and plenty of seasoning and mix well.

3 Put the turkey, breast side up, on a board. Use tweezers to pluck any feathers from the skin. Loosen the skin at the neck end and use your fingers to ease the skin away from the breast meat, until 9cm (3½in) is free. Spread most of the butter between the skin and meat. Put the remaining flavoured butter to one side.

4 Spoon the cold stuffing into the neck cavity, pushing it down between the skin and breast meat and taking care not to overfill. Neaten the shape. Turn

the turkey over on to its breast, pull the neck flap down and over the stuffing and secure the neck skin with a skewer or cocktail sticks. Weigh the turkey and calculate the cooking time, allowing 30–35 minutes per 1kg (2¼lb).

5 Make a platform in a large roasting tin with celery sticks and carrot halves and sit the turkey on top. Put the clementine halves and the remaining sage (sticks and all) into the turkey cavity, then rub the remaining flavoured butter over the breast of the bird. Tie the legs together with string, season the bird all over and cover loosely with foil.

6 Roast for the calculated time, removing the foil for the last 45 minutes of cooking, and basting at least three times during cooking. If the skin is browning too quickly, cover with foil again.

7 To check if the turkey is cooked, pierce the thickest part of the thigh with a skewer – the juices should run clear. If there are any traces of pink in the juice, put the bird back into the oven and cook for 10 minutes, then check again in the same way. Alternatively, use a meat thermometer – the temperature needs to read 78°C when inserted into the thickest part of the breast.

8 When the turkey is cooked, tip the bird so that the juices run into the tin,

then transfer the turkey to a board (put the tin for the Madeira Gravy to one side). Cover loosely with foil and clean teatowels to help keep the heat in. Leave to rest in a warm place for 30 minutes–1¼ hours.

9 To make the gravy, spoon off most of the fat from the roasting tin (leaving the vegetables in the tin). Put the tin over a medium heat and add the flour. Cook, stirring well with a wooden spoon, for 1 minute. Gradually add the Madeira, scraping up all the sticky bits from the bottom of the tin, then leave to bubble for a few minutes. Next, stir in the stock and leave to simmer, stirring occasionally, for 5 minutes. Check the seasoning and add the honey or redcurrant jelly if needed. Strain into a warmed gravy jug, or into a clean pan to reheat when needed.

10 To serve, unwrap the turkey and transfer to a warmed plate. Remove the skewer or cocktail sticks and garnish with the fried clementine halves and stuffing balls, if you like. Serve with the gravy.

Serves 8, with leftovers (see previous page)

Serves 8, with leftovers (see overleaf)

Lemon and Parsley Butter Roast Turkey

Hands-on time: 25 minutes
Cooking time: about 3½ hours, plus resting

5.4kg (12lb) free-range turkey (keep the giblets for stock to one side – see page 44. Spend as much as you can on your turkey – you'll notice the difference in the texture and taste)

1 lemon, zested (put the lemon to one side)

100g (3½oz) unsalted butter, softened

20g pack of fresh flat-leafed parsley, finely chopped

500g (1lb 2oz) uncooked Herbed Bread Stuffing (see page 59)

1 red onion, halved

5 fresh bay leaves (optional)

salt and freshly ground black pepper

fresh bay leaves and extra lemon halves browned (cut side down) in oil to garnish (optional)

1 Remove the turkey from the fridge 1 hour before you stuff it to let it come up to room temperature.

2 Preheat the oven to 190°C (170°C fan oven) mark 5. Put the lemon zest, butter, parsley and plenty of seasoning into a small bowl and mix well.

3 Put the turkey, breast side up, on a board. Use tweezers to pluck any feathers from the skin. Loosen the skin at the neck end and use your fingers to ease the skin gently away from breast meat, until about 9cm (3½in) is free. Spread the butter mixture between the skin and meat.

4 Spoon the cold stuffing into the neck cavity, pushing it down between the skin and breast meat and taking care not to overfill. Neaten the shape. Turn the turkey over on to its breast, pull the neck flap down and over the stuffing and secure the neck skin with a skewer or cocktail sticks. Weigh the

turkey and calculate the cooking time, allowing 30–35 minutes per 1kg (2¼lb)

5 Transfer the turkey to a large roasting tin. Cut the zested lemon in half and squeeze the juice over the bird. Put the juiced halves into the bird's cavity, together with the red onion halves and the bay leaves, if you like. Tie the legs together with string, season the bird all over and cover loosely with foil.

6 Roast for the calculated time, removing the foil for the last 30 minutes of cooking, and basting at least four times during cooking. If the skin is browning too quickly, cover with foil again.

7 To check if the turkey is cooked, pierce the thickest part of the thigh with a skewer – the juices should run clear. If there are any traces of pink in the juice, put the bird back into the oven and cook for 10 minutes, then check again in the same way. Alternatively, use a meat thermometer – the temperature needs to read 78°C when inserted into thickest part of the breast.

8 When the turkey is cooked, tip the bird so that the juices run into the tin, then transfer the turkey to a board (put the roasting tin for the gravy to one side). Cover well with foil and clean teatowels to help keep the heat in, then leave to rest in a warm place for 30 minutes–1¼ hours.

9 When ready to serve, put on a warmed plate or board, remove the string, skewer or cocktail sticks and garnish with bay leaves and lemon, if you like.

Top 5 Stuffings

Some people like moist stuffing, cooked inside the bird, while others prefer the crisper result when the stuffing is cooked in a separate dish – why not do half and half and please everyone? All these stuffings – with the exception of the wild rice stuffing – can be made a day ahead or frozen for up to one month. Thaw overnight in the fridge. Cook in a preheated oven, or alongside the roast.

Best-ever Sage and Onion Stuffing

To serve eight, you will need:
1 tbsp olive oil, 1 large very finely chopped onion, 2 tbsp finely chopped fresh sage, 7 heaped tbsp fresh white breadcrumbs, 900g (2lb) pork sausagemeat, 1 medium egg yolk, salt and freshly ground black pepper.

1 Heat the oil in a pan and gently fry the onion until soft and golden. Stir in the sage and leave to cool.
2 Keep 1 tbsp breadcrumbs to one side, then mix the remainder into the sausagemeat with the onion and egg yolk. Season with salt and ground black pepper, then leave to cool. Cover and chill overnight, or freeze.
3 Turn the stuffing out into an ovenproof dish, sprinkle with the reserved breadcrumbs and cook in an oven preheated to 180°C (160°C fan oven) mark 4 for 35–40 minutes until cooked through and golden.

Sausage, Cranberry and Apple Stuffing

To serve eight, you will need:
50g (2oz) butter, 1 finely chopped onion, 1 crushed garlic clove, 4 pork sausages (total weight about 275g/10oz), skinned and broken up, 75g (3oz) dried cranberries, 2 tbsp freshly chopped parsley, 1 red eating apple, salt and freshly ground black pepper.

1 Heat the butter in a pan, add the onion and cook over a medium heat for 5 minutes or until soft. Add the garlic and cook for 1 minute. Tip into a bowl and leave to cool. Add the sausages, cranberries and parsley, then cover and chill overnight, or freeze.

2 Core and chop the apple and add it to the stuffing. Season with salt and ground black pepper and stir well.

3 Turn the stuffing out into an ovenproof dish and cook in an oven preheated to 200°C (180°C fan oven) mark 6 for 30 minutes or until cooked through.

Fennel and Pinenut Stuffing

To serve eight, you will need:
75g (3oz) butter, plus extra for greasing, 1 bunch of spring onions, sliced, 450g (1lb) roughly chopped fennel, 4 tbsp freshly chopped tarragon, 50g (2oz) toasted pinenuts, 150g (5oz) goat's cheese, 150g (5oz) fresh breadcrumbs, 2 medium eggs, beaten, grated zest and juice of 1 lemon, salt and freshly ground black pepper.

1 Heat the butter in a pan, add the spring onions and cook for 3 minutes. Add the fennel and cook for 5 minutes, then leave to cool.

2 Add the tarragon, pinenuts, cheese, breadcrumbs, eggs, lemon zest and juice. Season with salt and ground black pepper and mix well. Cover and chill in the fridge overnight, or freeze.

3 Turn the stuffing out into a buttered ovenproof dish and cook in an oven preheated to 200°C (180°C fan oven) mark 6 for 30-40 minutes until golden.

Wild Rice and Cranberry Stuffing

This stuffing is great with goose. If you have the goose giblets, use the liver for this recipe.

To serve six to eight, you will need: 125g (4oz) wild rice, 225g (8oz) streaky bacon rashers, cut into short strips, 2 medium red onions (total weight about 225g/8oz), finely chopped, 75g (3oz) dried cranberries, 1 medium egg, beaten, salt and freshly ground black pepper and butter to grease.

1 Put the rice into a pan and cover with 900ml (1½ pints) cold water. Add ¼ tsp salt and bring to the boil. Reduce the heat and simmer, partly covered, for 45 minutes or until the rice is cooked. Drain and leave to cool.

2 Heat a large frying pan, add the bacon and dry-fry, turning from time to time, until lightly browned. Remove the bacon with a slotted spoon and transfer to a bowl. (If you have the goose liver, cook it in the same pan for 2–3 minutes, leave to cool, then chop it finely and add it to the bacon.) Add the onions to the frying pan and cook over a low heat until soft and translucent. Add the cranberries and cook for 1–2 minutes, then add the mixture to the bacon and leave to cool completely.

3 Add the cooked rice and the egg to the bacon mixture. Season with salt and ground black pepper, then stir thoroughly to combine. Cover and chill overnight.

4 Wrap the stuffing in a buttered piece of foil and cook in an oven preheated to 200°C (180°C fan oven) mark 6 for 30–40 minutes.

Herbed Bread Stuffing

To serve eight, you will need:
75g (3oz) butter, plus extra to dot,
1 finely chopped onion, 500g (1lb 2oz)
fresh white breadcrumbs,
1 tbsp dried mixed herbs, 500ml (17fl
oz) vegetable stock, 8 tbsp finely
chopped fresh mixed herbs, such as
parsley, thyme, sage and mint, plus
extra to garnish, 2 finely chopped,
celery sticks, 2 Braeburn apples, skin
on, cored and finely diced, 1 tbsp
ready toasted and chopped hazelnuts
and 4 smoked, streaky bacon rashers
(optional), salt and freshly ground
black pepper.

SAVE EFFORT

Prepare the stuffing to the end of step
2 up to 5 hours ahead. Put the 500g
(1lb 2oz) for the turkey to one side.
With the remaining stuffing, either
complete the recipe to the end of step
3, then cover and chill, or form into
balls, wrap in streaky bacon and put
on a baking tray. Cover and chill.
Complete step 4 to serve.

1 Heat the butter in a large frying
   pan, add the onion and cook
   gently for 10 minutes or until
   softened. Stir in the breadcrumbs
   and mix to combine. Next, add the
   dried herbs and pour in the stock.

2 Mix in the fresh herbs, celery,
   apples and hazelnuts and check
   the seasoning (don't stir too much
   or the mixture might go gluey).
   Put 500g (1lb 2oz) of the stuffing
   for the turkey to one side.

3 Spoon the remaining stuffing into
   an ovenproof serving dish (add
   some extra stock if you like your
   stuffing looser) and dot with some
   butter. Lay the bacon strips on top,
   if you like.

4 Cook in an oven preheated to
   190°C (170°C fan oven) mark 5 for
   30 minutes until the bacon is crisp
   and the stuffing is piping hot.
   Garnish with extra chopped herbs.

Perfect Roasting

To calculate the roasting time for the chicken see the chart on page 62. Test
if it is cooked by piercing the flesh with a skewer:
the juices should run clear.

Trussing

It is not necessary to truss poultry
before roasting it but it gives the bird
a neater shape for serving at the table.

1 To remove the wishbone, pull
   back the flap of skin at the neck
   end and locate the tip of the bone
   with a small sharp knife. Run the
   knife along the inside of the bone
   on both sides, then on the outside.
   Take care not to cut deep into
   the breast meat. Using poultry
   shears or sharp-pointed scissors,
   snip the tip of the bone from the
   breastbone and pull the bone away
   from the breast. Snip the two ends
   or pull them out by hand.

2 Put the wing tips under the breast and fold the neck flap on to the back of the bird. Thread a trussing needle and use it to secure the neck flap.

3 Push a metal skewer through both legs, at the joint between the thigh and drumstick. Twist some string around both ends of the skewer and pull firmly to tighten.

4 Turn the bird over. Bring the string over the ends of the drumsticks, pull tight and tie to secure the legs.

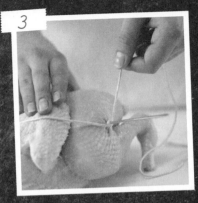

POULTRY AND GAME QUANTITIES FOR ROASTING

	SERVES
Chicken 2kg (4½lb)	about 5
Duck	allow 450g (1lb) per person
Goose 4.5kg (10lb)	6–8
Grouse	allow 1 bird per person
Guinea fowl	1 bird will serve 2–4
Partridge	allow 1 bird per person
Pheasant	1 bird will serve 2–3
Pigeon	allow 1 bird per person
Poussin	allow 1 bird per person
Quail	allow 2 birds per person
Turkey 3.5kg (7¾lb)	10
Woodcock	allow 1 bird per person

Poultry and game roasting times

CHICKEN

To calculate the roasting time for a chicken, weigh the oven-ready bird (including stuffing, if using) and allow 20 minutes per 450g (1lb) plus 20 minutes extra, in an oven preheated to 200°C (180°C fan oven) mark 6.

OVEN-READY WEIGHT	SERVES	COOKING TIME (APPROX.)
1.4-1.6 kg (3-3½lb)	4-6	1-1½ hours
1.8-2.3kg (4-5lb)	6-8	1 hour 50 minutes
2.5-2.7kg (5½-6lb)	8-10	2¼ hours

TURKEY

To calculate the roasting time for a turkey, weigh the oven-ready bird (including stuffing, if using) and allow 30-35 minutes per 1kg (2¼lb) (20 minutes per 450g (1lb), plus 20 minutes extra, in an oven preheated to 190°C (170°C fan oven) mark 5. Remove the foil about 1 hour before the end of cooking time to brown the bird. Baste regularly.

OVEN-READY WEIGHT (at room temperature)	SERVES (APPROX.)	THAWING TIME	COOKING TIME (foil-wrapped)
2.3-3.6kg (5-8lb)	4-8	15-18 hours	2-3 hours
3.6-5kg (8-11lb)	8-11	18-20 hours	3-3¼ hours
5-6.8kg (11-15lb)	11-15	20-24 hours	3¼-4 hours
6.8-9kg (15-20lb)	15-20	24-30 hours	4-5½ hours

OTHER POULTRY

These figures are a general guideline and recipes may vary. Preheat the oven to 200°C (180°C fan oven) mark 6.

	SERVES	COOKING TIME (APPROX.)
Poussin	1-2	20 minutes per 450g (1lb)
Guinea fowl 1.4kg (3lb)	3-4	1½ hours
Duck 1.8-2.5kg (4-5½lb)	2-4	1½-2 hours
Goose, small 3.6-5.4kg (8-12lb)	4-7	20 minutes per 450g (1lb)
Goose, medium 5.4-6.3kg (12-14lb)	8-11	25 minutes per 450g (1lb)

How to tell if poultry is cooked

To check if chicken or turkey is cooked, pierce the thickest part of the meat – usually the thigh – with a skewer. The juices that run out should be golden and clear with no traces of pink; if they're not, put the bird back into the oven and check at regular intervals.

Duck and game birds are traditionally served with the meat slightly pink: if overcooked, the meat may be dry.

Basting

Chicken, turkey and other poultry needs to be basted regularly during roasting to keep the flesh moist. Use an oven glove to steady the roasting tin and spoon the juices and melted fat over the top of the bird. Alternatively, use a bulb baster.

Resting times

Turkey and goose	up to 1¼ hours
Chicken and duck	15 minutes
Grouse and small game birds	10 minutes

Carving poultry

After resting, put the bird on a carving board.

1 Steady the bird with a carving fork. To cut breast meat, start at the neck end and cut slices about 5mm (¼in) thick. Use the carving knife and fork to lift them on to a warmed serving plate.

2 To cut off the legs, cut the skin between the thigh and breast.

3 Pull the leg down to expose the joint between the thigh bone and ribcage and cut through that joint.

4 Cut through the joint between the thigh and drumstick.

5 To carve meat from the leg (for turkeys and very large chickens), remove it from the carcass and joint the two parts of the leg, as above. Holding the drumstick by the thin end, stand it up on the carving board and carve slices roughly parallel with the bone. The thigh can be carved either flat on the board or upright.

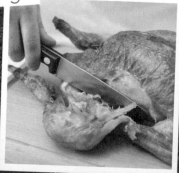

Poussins and small game birds

Poussins and other small birds such as grouse can serve one or two people. To serve two, you will need to split them. The easiest way to do this is with poultry shears and using a carving fork to steady the bird. Insert the shears between the legs and cut through the breastbone. As you do this the bird will open out, exposing the backbone; cut through the backbone.

Storing leftovers

Don't forget the leftovers when the meal is finished – never leave poultry standing in a warm room. Cool quickly in a cold place, then cover and chill.

Fruity Guinea Fowl

Slow Cooker Recipe

Hands-on time: 40 minutes, plus marinating
Cooking time: about 25 minutes in pan, then about 6 hours on Low

225g (8oz) onion, roughly chopped

125g (4oz) carrot, chopped

125g (4oz) celery, chopped

6–8 guinea fowl joints, total weight 2kg (4½lb)

750ml (1¼ pints) red wine

1 tsp black peppercorns, crushed

1 tbsp freshly chopped thyme

2 bay leaves

175g (6oz) ready-to-eat dried prunes

3 tbsp vegetable oil

225g (8oz) streaky bacon rashers, cut into strips

3 garlic cloves, crushed

1 tsp harissa paste

1 tbsp tomato purée

2 tbsp plain flour

300ml (½ pint) chicken stock (see page 44)

2 apples

salt and freshly ground black pepper

mashed potatoes to serve

1 Put the onion, carrot, celery, guinea fowl, 600ml (1 pint) of the wine, the peppercorns, thyme and bay leaves into a large bowl. Cover, chill and leave to marinate for at least 3–4 hours. Soak the prunes in the remaining wine for 3–4 hours.

2 Preheat the oven to 170°C (150°C fan oven) mark 3. Drain and dry the joints (put the vegetables and wine to one side). Heat 2 tbsp of the oil in a large pan. Brown the joints in batches, over a medium heat, then transfer to the slow cooker.

3 Add the marinated vegetables and the bacon to the pan (keep the marinade to one side) and stir-fry for 5 minutes. Add the garlic, harissa and tomato purée and cook for 1 minute. Mix in the flour and cook for 1 minute. Pour in the reserved marinade and stock and bring to the boil, stirring, then pour into the slow cooker and season well. Cover and cook on Low for 4–6 hours until the guinea fowl is cooked through.

4 Heat the remaining oil in a pan. Core and slice the apples, then cook for 2-3 minutes on each side until golden. Put to one side.

5 Remove the joints from the slow cooker. Strain the sauce and put back into the slow cooker with the joints. Add the prunes and any juices and the apple. Leave to stand for 10 minutes. Serve with mashed potatoes.

WITHOUT A SLOW COOKER

Complete step 1. In step 2, put the joints to one side after browning, then continue with step 3 until you pour in the reserved marinade and stock. Bring to the boil, then season well, cover and cook in the oven for 40 minutes. Complete steps 4 and 5, pouring the sauces back into the casserole instead of the slow cooker. Heat through in the oven for 10 minutes before serving.

Serves 6

Goose with Roasted Apples

Hands-on time: 30 minutes
Cooking time: 3 hours, plus resting

6 small red onions, halved

7 small red eating apples, unpeeled,
halved

5kg (11lb) oven-ready goose, dried and
seasoned inside and out

1 small bunch of fresh sage

1 small bunch of fresh rosemary

1 bay leaf

salt and freshly ground black pepper

For the gravy

1 tbsp plain flour

300ml (½ pint) red wine

200ml (7fl oz) giblet stock (see page 45)

1 Preheat the oven to 230°C (210°C fan
oven) mark 8. Put half an onion and
half an apple inside the goose with
half the sage and rosemary and the
bay leaf. Tie the legs together with
string. Push a long skewer through
the wings to tuck them in. Put the
goose, breast side up, on a rack in a
roasting tin. Prick the breast all over
and season with salt and ground black

pepper. Put the remaining onions
around the bird, then cover loosely
with foil.

2 Roast in the oven for 30 minutes, then
take the tin out of the oven and baste
the goose with the fat that has run off.
Remove and put any excess fat to one
side. Reduce the oven temperature
to 190°C (170°C fan oven) mark 5 and
roast for a further 1½ hours, removing
any excess fat every 20-30 minutes.

3 Remove the foil from the goose.
Remove excess fat from the tin, then
add the remaining apples. Sprinkle
the goose with the remaining herbs
and roast for a further 1 hour or until
cooked. To test if the bird is cooked,
pierce the thickest part of the thigh
with a skewer – the juices should run
clear. If there are any traces of pink
in the juice, put the bird back into
the oven and cook for 10 minutes,
then check again in the same way.
Alternatively, use a meat thermometer
– the temperature needs to read 78°C

when inserted into the thickest part of the breast.

4 Take the goose out of the oven and put it on a warmed serving plate. Cover with foil and leave to rest for 30 minutes. Remove the apples and onions and keep warm.

5 To make the gravy, pour out all but 1 tbsp of the fat from the tin, stir in the flour, then add the wine and stock. Bring to the boil and cook, stirring, for 5 minutes.

6 Carve the goose, cut the roast apples into wedges and serve with the goose, onions and gravy.

Serves 6–8

Meaty Dishes

Great Big Pork Pie

Hands-on time: 30 minutes, plus overnight chilling
Cooking time: about 1 hour 20 minutes, plus cooling

For the pastry

vegetable oil to grease

900g (2lb) plain flour, plus extra to dust

1 tsp salt

250g (9oz) lard

For the filling

½ tbsp vegetable oil

1 onion, finely chopped

1kg (2¼lb) pork mince

6 smoked streaky bacon rashers, cut into 1cm (½in) pieces

¼ tsp mixed spice

a small handful of fresh parsley, finely chopped

½ tsp salt

4 tbsp onion marmalade

1 medium egg, beaten

100ml (3½fl oz) chicken stock (see page 44)

1 sheet leaf gelatine

freshly ground black pepper

1 Grease a 20.5cm (8in) springform cake tin with oil and put on a large baking tray. To make the pastry, put the flour and salt into a food processor. Next, melt the lard and 300ml (½ pint) water in a small pan and bring to the boil. With the motor of the processor running, add the hot lard mixture and whiz until the pastry nearly comes together. Tip on to a worksurface, bring together with your hands and knead until smooth.

2 Break off two-thirds of the pastry (put the remaining one-third to one side, uncovered) and roll out on a lightly floured surface until about 1cm (½in) thick. Use to line the prepared tin, leaving some pastry hanging over the sides. Chill for 10 minutes. Cover the remaining pastry and put to one side at room temperature.

3 Preheat the oven to 180°C (160°C fan oven) mark 4. To make the filling, heat the oil in a small frying pan and gently cook the onion for 8 minutes

until softened. Tip into a large bowl and leave to cool for a couple of minutes, then mix in the mince, bacon, mixed spice, parsley, ½ tsp salt and lots of ground black pepper.

4 Tip half the filling into the chilled pastry case and pat down firmly. Spread the onion marmalade over the filling and top with the remaining filling, pressing down as before.

5 Roll out the remaining pastry as before until large enough to cover the pie. Place on top of the filling, then trim and crimp the edges (ensure the crimped edge sits inside the perimeter of the tin or the pie will be hard to remove). Brush the top with some of the beaten egg (don't brush the outer edge of the crimping as the egg will make the pastry stick to the tin).

6 Bake for 40 minutes, then carefully unclip and remove the outside ring of the tin, leaving the pie on its base on the baking tray. Brush all over with egg and put back into the oven for 30–35 minutes to set the sides and cook through. Take out of the oven.

7 Pour the cold stock into a pan and add the gelatine leaf. Leave to soak for 5 minutes, then heat gently until the gelatine dissolves. Empty into a jug.

8 Filling the pie with the stock mixture isn't an essential step, but there'll be a gap between the meat and pastry if you don't. Use the tip of a knife or a skewer to poke a small hole in the top of the pie. Using a fine funnel (or a steady hand), pour a little stock into the hole and wait for it to be absorbed. Keep adding stock (and waiting for it to be absorbed) until the pie will take no more. Leave the pie to cool for 30 minutes, then chill overnight. Allow to come up to room temperature before serving.

Cuts into 12 slices

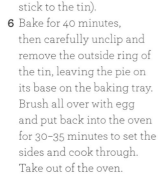

Veal and Ham Pie

Hands-on time: 45 minutes, plus chilling
Cooking time: about 3½ hours, plus cooling

3 or 4 small veal bones

1 small onion

1 bay leaf

4 black peppercorns

700g (1½lb) diced pie veal

225g (8oz) diced cooked ham

1 tbsp freshly chopped flat-leafed parsley

grated zest and juice of 1 lemon

1 tbsp salt

½ tsp pepper

150ml (¼ pint) milk and 150ml (¼ pint) water mixed

150g (5oz) lard

450g (1lb) plain flour, plus extra to dust

1 medium egg, hard-boiled

1 medium egg, beaten

salad to serve

1 Put the bones, onion, bay leaf and peppercorns into a pan and cover with water. Simmer for 20 minutes, then boil to reduce the liquid to 150ml (¼ pint). Strain and cool. Base-line a 20.5cm (8in) springform cake tin.

2 Mix together the diced veal, diced ham, parsley, lemon zest and juice, 1 tsp salt and the pepper.

3 Bring the milk and water and the lard to the boil in a pan, then gradually beat it into the flour and remaining salt in a bowl. Knead for 3–4 minutes.

4 Roll out two-thirds of the pastry on a lightly floured surface and mould into the springform cake tin. Cover and chill for 30 minutes. Keep the remaining pastry covered. Preheat the oven to 220°C (200°C fan oven) mark 7.

5 Spoon half the meat mixture and 2 tbsp cold jellied stock into the pastry case. Put the hard-boiled egg in the centre and cover with the remaining meat mixture and 2 more tbsp cold jellied stock. Roll out the remaining pastry to make a lid and put on top of the meat mixture, sealing the pastry edges well. Decorate with pastry trimmings and make a hole in the centre. Glaze with the beaten egg.

6 Bake for 30 minutes. Cover loosely with foil, reduce the oven temperature to 180°C (160°C fan oven) mark 4 and bake for a further 2½ hours. Cool.

7 Warm the remaining jellied stock until liquid, then pour into the centre hole of the pie. Chill the pie, then unmould and serve with salad.

FREEZE AHEAD

To make ahead and freeze, complete the recipe, then freeze the cooked pie whole, or in slices, wrapped in clingfilm for up to one month (wrapped slices can be stacked on top of each other). To serve, thaw in the fridge or at cool room temperature.

Cuts into 12 slices

Spicy Pork and Bean Stew

Hands-on time: 15 minutes
Cooking time: about 30 minutes in pan, then about 4 hours on Low

3 tbsp olive oil

400g (14oz) pork tenderloin, cubed

1 red onion, sliced

2 leeks, trimmed and cut into chunks

2 celery sticks, trimmed and cut
    into chunks

½ tbsp harissa paste

1 tbsp tomato purée

400g can cherry tomatoes

150ml (¼ pint) hot vegetable or chicken
    stock (see page 44)

400g can cannellini beans, drained
    and rinsed

1 marinated red pepper, sliced

salt and freshly ground black pepper

freshly chopped flat-leafed parsley
    to garnish

Greek yogurt, lemon wedges and
    wholegrain bread to serve

1 Heat 2 tbsp of the oil in a large pan.
   Add the pork and fry in batches until
   golden. Transfer to the slow cooker.

2 Heat the remaining oil in the pan.
   Add the onion and fry for 5–10
   minutes until softened. Add the leeks
   and celery and cook for 5 minutes.
   Add the harissa and tomato purée and
   cook for 1–2 minutes, stirring all the
   time. Add the tomatoes and hot stock
   and season well. Bring to the boil, then
   pour into the slow cooker, cover and
   cook on Low for 3–4 hours.

3 Stir in the drained beans and red
   pepper and leave to stand for 5
   minutes to warm through. Garnish
   with parsley and serve with a dollop
   of yogurt, a grinding of black pepper,
   lemon wedges for squeezing over the
   stew, and chunks of crusty baguette or
   wholegrain bread.

Complete steps 1 and 2, but fry the pork in a flameproof casserole. In step 2, bring to the boil, then transfer to the oven and cook for 25 minutes. Complete step 3 to finish the recipe.

SAVE EFFORT

For an easy way to get a brand new dish, instead of pork, use the same quantity of lean lamb, such as leg, trimmed of excess fat and then cut into cubes.

Serves 4

Perfect Ham

Hams come in different sizes and cures. Some are sold cooked, others are uncooked. Some need to be soaked, so buy your ham from a butcher and ask his advice on preparation and cooking.

Preparing and cooking ham

1 If the ham needs to be soaked, place it in a large container that will hold it comfortably with plenty of space for water. Pour cold water over it to cover and weigh down the ham if necessary. Leave to soak overnight, then drain well.

2 Put the ham into a large flameproof casserole and cover with cold water. Add a few sprigs of parsley, a few peppercorns, a bay leaf and a chopped onion to the water, if you like. Bring to just below boiling point – do not let the water boil or the meat will be tough. Skim off any surface scum. Simmer gently for 25 minutes per 450g (1lb), checking occasionally to make sure it is completely covered with water.

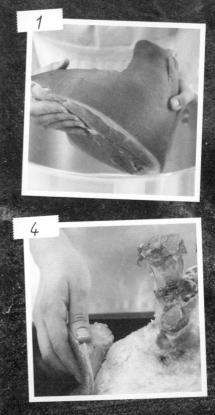

3 Leave to cool in the water. Transfer
   the ham to a roasting tin. (Put the
   stock for soup to one side.)

4 Preheat the oven to 200°C (180°C
   fan oven) mark 6. Remove the
   rind and neatly trim the fat so that
   there is a 5mm–1cm (¼–½in) layer
   left on the meat.

5 Score the fat with parallel lines
   about 5cm (2in) apart, then score
   on the diagonal to make diamond
   shapes. Press a clove into the
   centre of each diamond.

6 Spread prepared English mustard
   thinly and evenly over the ham
   – or glaze as the recipe suggests.
   Sprinkle with soft brown sugar
   to make a light but even coating.
   Bake the ham for about
   30 minutes until golden brown.

Ginger and Honey-glazed Ham

Hands-on time: about 30 minutes
Cooking time: 5¾ hours

4.5–6.8kg (10–15lb) unsmoked gammon
    on the bone

2 shallots, halved

6 cloves

3 bay leaves

2 celery sticks, cut into 5cm (2in) pieces

2 tbsp prepared English mustard

5cm (2in) piece fresh root ginger, peeled
    and thinly sliced

For the glaze

225g (8oz) dark brown sugar

2 tbsp runny honey

8 tbsp brandy or Madeira

For the chutney

4 mangoes, peeled, sliced and chopped
    into 5cm (2in) chunks

1 tsp mixed spice

4 cardamom pods, seeds removed and
    crushed

½ tsp ground cinnamon

4 tbsp raisins

1 Put the gammon into a large pan.
   Add the shallots, cloves, bay leaves
   and celery and enough cold water to
   cover. Bring to the boil, then cover,
   reduce the heat and simmer gently for
   about 5 hours. Remove any scum with
   a slotted spoon. Lift the ham out of the
   pan, discard the vegetables and herbs
   and leave to cool.

2 Preheat the oven to 200°C (180°C fan
   oven) mark 6. Using a sharp knife,
   carefully cut away the ham's thick
   skin to leave an even layer of fat. Score
   a diamond pattern in the fat and put
   the ham into a roasting tin. Smother
   evenly with the mustard and tuck the
   ginger into the scored fat.

3 To make the glaze, put the sugar,
   honey and brandy or Madeira into
   a pan and heat until the sugar has
   dissolved. Brush over the ham.

4 Mix all the chutney ingredients in a
   bowl, add any remaining glaze, then
   spoon around the ham.

5 Cook the ham for 30–40 minutes, basting every 10 minutes. Remove the ham from the roasting tin and put to one side. Stir the chutney and put it under the grill for 5 minutes to allow the mango to caramelise. Transfer the chutney to a side dish and serve with the ham.

Serves 8–10

Cumberland Glazed Baked Gammon

Hands-on time: 30 minutes
Cooking time: about 4¼ hours

4.5kg (10lb) smoked gammon joint, on the bone

2 celery sticks, roughly chopped

1 onion, quartered

1 carrot, roughly chopped

1 tsp black peppercorns

1 tbsp cloves

75g (3oz) redcurrant sprigs

For the Cumberland glaze

grated zest and juice of ½ lemon and ½ orange

4 tbsp redcurrant jelly

1 tsp Dijon mustard

2 tbsp port

salt and freshly ground black pepper

1 Put the gammon into a large pan. Add the celery, onion, carrot and peppercorns. Cover the meat and vegetables with cold water and bring to the boil, then cover, reduce the heat and simmer for 2¾–3½ hours or allowing 15–20 minutes per 450g (1lb) plus 15 minutes. Lift the gammon out of the pan. Preheat the oven to 200°C (180°C fan oven) mark 6.

2 Meanwhile, make the glaze. Heat the lemon and orange zests and juices, redcurrant jelly, mustard and port in a pan to dissolve the jelly. Bring to the boil and bubble for 5 minutes or until syrupy. Season with salt and ground black pepper to taste.

3 Remove the gammon rind and score the fat in a diamond pattern. Put the gammon into a roasting tin, then stud the fat with the cloves. Spoon the glaze evenly over the gammon joint.

4 Roast the gammon for 40 minutes, basting the meat with any juices. Add the redcurrant sprigs 10 minutes before the end of the cooking time. Serve the gammon hot or cold, carved into thin slices, with the redcurrant sprigs.

Serves 16

Pork and Apple Hotpot

🍴 **Hands-on time:** 15 minutes
Cooking time: about 2¼ hours

1 tbsp olive oil

900g (2lb) pork shoulder steaks

3 onions, cut into wedges

1 large Bramley apple, peeled, cored and thickly sliced

1 tbsp plain flour

600ml (1 pint) hot weak vegetable or chicken stock (see page 44)

¼ Savoy cabbage, sliced

2 fresh thyme sprigs

900g (2lb) large potatoes, cut into 2cm (¾in) slices

25g (1oz) butter

salt and freshly ground black pepper

1 Preheat the oven to 170°C (150°C fan oven) mark 3. Heat the oil in a large non-stick flameproof casserole until very hot, then fry the steaks, two at a time, for 5 minutes or until golden all over. Remove the steaks from the pan and put to one side.

2 In the same casserole, fry the onions for 10 minutes or until soft – add a little water if they start to stick. Stir in the apple and cook for 1 minute, then add the flour to soak up the juices. Gradually add the hot stock and stir until smooth. Season, then stir in the cabbage and add the pork. Throw in the thyme, overlap the potato slices on top, then dot with the butter.

3 Cover with a tight-fitting lid and cook near the top of the oven for 1 hour. Remove the lid and cook for 30–45 minutes until the potatoes are tender and golden. Put the hotpot under the grill for 2–3 minutes to crisp up the potatoes, if you like.

FREEZE AHEAD

If you are going to freeze this dish, then use a freezerproofcasserole. Complete the recipe, cool quickly, then freeze in the casserole for up to three months. To use, thaw overnight at cool room temperature.

Preheat the oven to 180°C (160°C fan oven) mark 4. Pour 50ml (2fl oz) hot stock over the hotpot, then cover and reheat for 30 minutes or until piping hot. Uncover and crisp the potatoes under the grill for 2–3 minutes.

Serves 4

Perfect Roast Pork

Loin of pork produces wonderfully crisp crackling, but many other pork joints are also suitable for roasting; from quick-cooking fillet to pork belly, which requires long, slow roasting for melt-in-the-mouth succulence.

Crackling and carving
Perfect crackling

- [ ] If possible, ask the butcher to score the skin for you
- [ ] The pork skin needs to be dry. Remove the shop's wrapping and pat the skin dry with some kitchen paper
- [ ] Leave the joint uncovered in the fridge overnight to dry out the skin
- [ ] If the skin hasn't been scored, use a craft knife or your sharpest knife to score the skin, cutting about halfway into the fat underneath
- [ ] Rub the scored skin with a little olive oil and salt
- [ ] Once cooked, if your crackling isn't as crispy as you'd like, you can still rescue it. Preheat the grill to medium-high. Remove the crackling from the meat and put the whole piece on to a baking tray. Grill until crisp and puffed (watch carefully to avoid scorching, turning the tray to avoid any hot spots)

Carving pork with crackling

1 It is much easier to slice cooked pork if you first remove the crackling. Remove any string and position the carving knife just under the skin on the topmost side of the joint. Work the knife under the crackling, taking care not to cut into the meat, until you can pull it off with your fingers.

2 Slice the meat, then snap the crackling into servings.

1

4

Perfect Roast Pork Belly

Hands-on time: 15 minutes, plus drying
Cooking time: about 3½ hours, plus resting

1.5kg (3lb 2oz) piece pork belly
salt

1 Using a small sharp knife, score lines into the skin (cutting into the fat) about 1cm (½in) apart, but not so deep that you cut into the meat. Pat the pork completely dry, then leave uncovered at room temperature to air dry for about 45 minutes.

2 Preheat the oven to 220°C (200°C fan oven) mark 7. Rub lots of salt over the pork skin. Rest a wire rack in a deep roasting tin and put the pork, skin side up, on the rack. Roast for 30 minutes, then reduce the oven temperature to 170°C (150°C fan oven) mark 3 and continue cooking for 3 hours – by this stage the crackling should be crisp and golden (if not, don't panic, crisp it up under the grill – see page 86).

3 Transfer the pork to a board and, using a sharp knife, slice off the crackling in one piece (about the outer 2cm/¾in). Cover the pork meat loosely with foil and leave to rest for 30–40 minutes.

4 Cut the crackling into six long strips, then cut the pork belly into six neat squares. Serve each square topped with a strip of crackling.

Serves 6

Beef and
Lamb Dishes

Parson's Venison

Hands-on time: 10 minutes, plus overnight marinating
Cooking time: about 2½ hours, plus cooling

25g (1oz) butter

1 small onion, finely chopped

125g (4oz) mushrooms, chopped

125g (4oz) cooked ham, chopped

2 tbsp snipped fresh chives

1.8–2kg (4–4½lb) leg of lamb, boned

salt and freshly ground black pepper

For the marinade

200ml (7fl oz) dry red wine

75ml (2½fl oz) port

6 juniper berries, crushed

¼ tsp ground allspice

3 tbsp red wine vinegar

1 bay leaf

¼ tsp freshly grated nutmeg

1 Melt half the butter in a pan. Add the onion and mushrooms and cook, stirring frequently, until the onion is soft but not browned. Stir in the ham and chives and season to taste. Leave to cool.

2 Season the lamb inside and out with ground black pepper, then spread the onion mixture over the inside. Roll up tightly and tie securely. Put the lamb in a large glass bowl or casserole.

3 Mix all the ingredients for the marinade. Pour over the lamb, cover and leave in a cool place for 24 hours, turning occasionally.

4 The next day, preheat the oven to 180°C (160°C fan oven) mark 4. Remove the meat from the marinade, drain and dry. Put the marinade to one side. Melt the remaining butter in a flameproof casserole. Add the meat and brown on all sides over a medium-high heat.

5 Pour in the marinade and bring almost to the boil, then cover and cook in the oven for 1¾–2 hours until the meat is tender, basting occasionally with the marinade.

6 Transfer the meat to a warmed plate. Skim the fat from the surface of the liquid, then boil rapidly until syrupy. Remove the bay leaf, adjust the seasoning and serve with the meat.

Serves 6

Lamb and Orzo Stew

Hands-on time: 10 minutes
Cooking time: about 2 hours

1 tbsp vegetable oil

1kg (2¼lb) diced lamb (leg or shoulder), excess fat trimmed

2 red onions, finely sliced

1 tbsp dried oregano

1 tsp ground cinnamon

400g can chopped tomatoes

1.2 litres (2¼ pints) vegetable stock

200g (7oz) orzo pasta

50g (2oz) pitted black olives, roughly chopped

a large handful of fresh parsley, roughly chopped

salt and freshly ground black pepper

1 Heat the oil in a large heatproof casserole dish or pan and brown the lamb in batches. Once all the meat is browned, lift out and put to one side on a plate.

2 Put the casserole/pan back onto the heat, add the onions and cook gently for 10 minutes or until softened (add a little water if the pan looks too dry). Stir in the oregano and cinnamon and cook for 1 minute, then stir in the tomatoes, stock and lamb. Cover and simmer for 1¼ hours, stirring occasionally, or until the lamb is tender.

3 Stir the orzo into the casserole/pan and cook, uncovered, for a further 10–12 minutes until the orzo is tender. (Once the orzo is tender, it will continue to swell on standing. If you're not serving it immediately, add a little extra water until the desired consistency is reached.) Next, stir in the olives and most of the parsley. Check the seasoning and garnish with the remaining parsley. Serve immediately.

Serves 6

Lamb and Barley Stew

Hands-on time: 15 minutes
Cooking time: 2½ hours

2 tbsp plain wholemeal flour

1.4kg (3lb) boned leg or shoulder of lamb, trimmed of fat and cubed

3 streaky bacon rashers, rind removed

25g (1oz) butter

2 medium onions, chopped

2 medium carrots, sliced

125g (4oz) turnip or swede, diced

2 celery sticks, diced

2 tbsp pearl barley

2 tsp mixed freshly chopped herbs, such as thyme, rosemary, parsley, basil

300ml (½ pint) lamb or beef stock

salt and freshly ground black pepper

freshly chopped flat-leafed parsley to garnish

1 Season the flour with salt and ground black pepper, then toss the lamb in the flour.

2 Dry-fry the bacon in a large flameproof casserole until the fat runs. Add the butter and lamb and fry until browned all over, stirring. Using a slotted spoon, remove the lamb and bacon from the casserole and put to one side.

3 Add the onions, carrots, turnip or swede and the celery to the casserole and fry for 5–10 minutes until beginning to brown.

4 Put the lamb back into the casserole, add the pearl barley and herbs and pour in the stock. Bring to the boil, then reduce the heat, cover and simmer for 2 hours, stirring occasionally to prevent sticking, or until the lamb is tender.

5 Serve hot, sprinkled with parsley.

Serves 6

Luxury Lamb and Leek Hotpot

Hands-on time: 20 minutes
Cooking time: 2¾ hours

50g (2oz) butter

400g (14oz) leeks, trimmed and sliced

1 medium onion, chopped

1 tbsp olive oil

800g (1¾lb) casserole lamb, cubed and tossed with 1 tbsp plain flour

2 garlic cloves, crushed

800g (1¾lb) waxy potatoes, such as Desiree, sliced

3 tbsp freshly chopped flat-leafed parsley

1 tsp freshly chopped thyme

300ml (½ pint) lamb stock

142ml carton double cream

salt and freshly ground black pepper

1 Melt half the butter in a 3.5 litre (6¼ pint) flameproof casserole. Add the leeks and onion and stir to coat, then cover and cook over a low heat for 10 minutes. Transfer the leeks and onion on to a large sheet of greaseproof paper.

2 Heat the oil in the casserole, then brown the lamb in batches with the garlic and plenty of salt and ground black pepper. Remove and put to one side on another large sheet of greaseproof paper.

3 Preheat the oven to 170°C (150°C fan oven) mark 3. Put half the potatoes in a layer over the bottom of the casserole and season. Add the meat, then spoon the leek mixture on top. Arrange a layer of overlapping potatoes on top of that, sprinkle with herbs, then pour in the stock.

4 Bring the casserole to the boil, then cover and transfer to a low shelf in the oven and cook for about 1 hour 50 minutes. Take out of the oven, dot with the remaining butter and add the cream. Put back into the oven and cook, uncovered, for 30–40 minutes until the potatoes are golden brown.

Serves 6

Irish Stew

Hands-on time: 15 minutes
Cooking time: about 2¼ hours

700g (1½lb) middle neck lamb cutlets, fat trimmed

2 onions, thinly sliced

450g (1lb) potatoes, thinly sliced

1 tbsp freshly chopped flat-leafed parsley, plus extra to garnish

1 tbsp dried thyme

300ml (½ pint) hot lamb stock

salt and freshly ground black pepper

1 Preheat the oven to 170°C (150°C fan oven) mark 3. Layer the meat, onions and potatoes in a deep casserole dish, sprinkling some herbs and salt and ground black pepper between each layer. Finish with a layer of potato, overlapping the slices neatly.

2 Pour the hot stock over the potatoes, then cover with greaseproof paper and a lid. Cook in the oven for about 2 hours until the meat is tender.

3 Preheat the grill. Take the lid off the casserole and remove the paper. Put under the grill and brown the top of the potatoes. Sprinkle with chopped parsley and serve immediately.

Serves 4

Braised Oxtail

Hands-on time: 20 minutes
Cooking time: about 4½ hours

2 oxtails (total weight about 1.6kg/3½lb), trimmed

2 tbsp plain flour

4 tbsp oil

2 large onions, sliced

900ml (1½ pints) beef stock

150ml (¼ pint) red wine

1 tbsp tomato purée

finely grated zest of ½ lemon

2 bay leaves

2 medium carrots, chopped

450g (1lb) parsnips, chopped

salt and freshly ground black pepper

freshly chopped flat-leafed parsley to garnish

1 Cut the oxtails into large pieces. Put the flour into a plastic bag, season with salt and ground black pepper, then toss the meat in it. Heat the oil in a large flameproof casserole and brown the oxtail pieces, a few at a time. Remove from the casserole with a slotted spoon and put to one side.

2 Add the onions to the casserole and fry over a medium heat for about 10 minutes until softened and lightly browned. Stir in any remaining flour.

3 Stir in the stock, red wine, tomato purée, lemon zest and bay leaves and season with salt and ground black pepper. Bring to the boil, then put the oxtail back into the casserole and reduce the heat. Cover and simmer very gently for 2 hours.

4 Skim off the fat from the surface, then stir in the carrots and parsnips. Re-cover the casserole and simmer very gently for a further 2 hours or until the oxtail is very tender.

5 Skim off all the fat from the surface, then check the seasoning. Serve scattered with chopped parsley.

Serves 6

Peppered Winter Stew

Hands-on time: 20 minutes
Cooking time: about 2¾ hours

25g (1oz) plain flour

900g (2lb) stewing venison, beef or lamb, cut into 4cm (1½in) cubes

5 tbsp vegetable or olive oil

225g (8oz) whole button onions or shallots

225g (8oz) onion, finely chopped

4 garlic cloves, crushed

2 tbsp tomato purée

125ml (4fl oz) red wine vinegar

750ml bottle red wine

2 tbsp redcurrant jelly

1 small bunch of fresh thyme, plus extra sprigs to garnish (optional)

4 bay leaves

6 cloves

900g (2lb) mixed root vegetables, such as carrots, parsnips, turnips and celeriac, cut into 4cm (1½in) chunks; carrots cut a little smaller

600–900ml (1–1½ pints) beef stock

salt and freshly ground black pepper

1 Preheat the oven to 180°C (160°C fan oven) mark 4. Put the flour into a plastic bag, season with salt and ground black pepper, then toss the meat in it.

2 Heat 3 tbsp of the oil in a large flameproof casserole over a medium heat and brown the meat well in small batches. Remove and put to one side.

3 Heat the remaining oil and fry the button onions or shallots for 5 minutes or until golden. Add the chopped onion and the garlic and cook, stirring, until soft and golden. Add the tomato purée and cook for a further 2 minutes, then add the vinegar and wine and bring to the boil. Bubble for 10 minutes.

4 Add the redcurrant jelly, thyme, bay leaves, 1 tbsp coarsely ground black pepper, the cloves and meat to the pan, with the vegetables and enough stock to barely cover the meat and vegetables. Bring to the boil, then reduce the heat, cover the pan and cook in the oven for 1¾–2¼ hours until the meat is very tender. Serve hot, garnished with thyme sprigs, if you like.

Serves 6

Perfect Roasting

Succulent roasts are simple when you know how. Once the joint is cooked to your liking, make sure it has time to rest before carving to allow the juices to redistribute themselves throughout the meat to give moist, tender results.

Roasting know-how

- ❑ Bring the meat to room temperature before cooking – remove from the fridge 1–2 hours ahead
- ❑ Cook on a wire rack, or on a bed of sliced vegetables, so that the fat drops away
- ❑ Roast fat side up
- ❑ During cooking, check the juices in the roasting tin to make sure they don't dry up and scorch – this will ruin the gravy. Pour a little freshly boiled water into the roasting tin if necessary
- ❑ When cooked, transfer the meat to a plate or dish, cover loosely with foil and leave to rest before carving. This makes the meat juicier and easier to carve. Allow the meat to rest for at least 15 minutes. A large joint can rest for 45 minutes without getting cold

Seasoning

All joints can be seasoned before roasting for extra flavour. Use salt and freshly ground black pepper, or a dry marinade (see below).

1 Rub the joint with vegetable oil to help the seasonings stick.
2 Press on the seasonings in a thin, uniform layer.

Dry marinades

These don't penetrate far into the meat, but give an excellent flavour on and just under the crust. Make them with crushed garlic, dried herbs or spices, and plenty of freshly ground black pepper. Rub into the meat and marinate in the fridge for at least 30 minutes or up to 8 hours.

Roast Rib of Beef

Hands-on time: 5 minutes
Cooking time: about 2¾ hours, plus resting

2-bone rib of beef (weight about 2.5–2.7kg/ (5½–6lb)

1 tbsp plain flour

1 tbsp English mustard powder

150ml (¼ pint) red wine

600ml (1 pint) beef stock

salt and freshly ground black pepper

fresh thyme sprigs to garnish

Yorkshire puddings, roasted root vegetables and a green vegetable to serve

1 Preheat the oven to 230°C (210°C fan oven) mark 8. Put the beef, fat side up, in a roasting tin just large enough to hold the joint. Mix the flour and mustard together in a small bowl and season with salt and ground black pepper, then rub the mixture over the beef. Roast in the centre of the oven for 30 minutes.

2 Move the beef to a lower shelf, near the bottom of the oven. Reduce the oven temperature to 220°C (200°C fan oven) mark 7 and continue to roast the beef for a further 2 hours, basting occasionally.

3 Transfer the beef to a carving dish, cover loosely with foil and leave to rest while you make the gravy. Skim off most of the fat from the roasting tin. Put the roasting tin on the hob over a high heat, pour in the wine and boil vigorously until very syrupy. Pour in the stock, bring to the boil and, again, boil until syrupy. Add 600ml (1 pint) vegetable water and boil until syrupy. There should be about 450ml (¾ pint) gravy. Taste and adjust the seasoning.

4 Remove the rib bone and carve the beef. Garnish with thyme and serve with the gravy, Yorkshire puddings and roasted vegetables.

SAVE TIME

Buy the best quality meat you can afford. The beef should be a dark red colour, not bright red, and have a good marbling of fat.

Serves 8

Perfect Cold Roast Beef

Hands-on time: 15 minutes, plus overnight chilling
Cooking time: about 2 hours

2kg (4½lb) rolled topside beef
　　roasting joint
2 tbsp light brown soft sugar
1 tbsp English mustard powder
1 tbsp vegetable oil
coleslaw, watercress leaves and creamed
　　horseradish to serve

1 Take the beef out of the fridge 1 hour before cooking to allow it to come up to room temperature.

2 Preheat the oven to 200°C (180°C fan oven) mark 6. Pat the beef dry with kitchen paper and take a note of its weight (just in case). Mix the sugar and mustard powder in a small bowl and rub over the beef. Heat the oil in a large frying pan over a high heat and fry the beef on all sides, until well browned.

3 Sit the beef in a roasting tin just large enough to hold the joint and cover loosely with foil. Roast in the oven for 15 minutes per 500g (1lb 2oz) for rare meat, 20 minutes per 500g (1lb 2oz) for medium-rare meat or 25 minutes per 500g (1lb 2oz) for well-done meat, then roast for an extra 10 minutes on top of the calculated time. Or use a meat thermometer – for medium-rare meat the internal temperature of the beef should be 60°C.

4 Transfer the beef to a board and leave to cool completely. Wrap well in foil and chill overnight. (You can also serve this beef hot as part of a Sunday lunch – just leave it to rest for 30 minutes after roasting, then carve.)

5 An hour before serving, slice the beef thinly and arrange on a serving plate, then cover. Serve with coleslaw, watercress leaves and creamed horseradish.

SAVE TIME

Cook the beef to the end of step 3 up to 3 days ahead, then complete the recipe and chill.

Serves 8

Perfect Braising and Pot-roasting

Tougher cuts require slow cooking. Braises and pot roasts are similar but braises need more liquid.

Tips for perfect results

- ❑ Good cuts of beef include shin, chuck, blade, brisket and flank; good cuts of lamb include leg, shoulder, neck, breast and shank
- ❑ Cuts you would normally roast can also be casseroled. These simply need less time in the oven
- ❑ Always use a low heat and check regularly to make sure that there is enough liquid to keep the meat from catching on the bottom of casserole
- ❑ Braises often improve by being cooked in advance and then gently reheated before serving. If you've braised a whole piece of meat, you can slice it before reheating

Braised Lamb Shanks

To serve six, you will need:
3 tbsp olive oil, 6 lamb shanks, 1 large
onion, 3 carrots, 3 celery sticks, all
thickly sliced, 2 crushed garlic cloves,
2 × 400g cans chopped tomatoes,
150ml (¼ pint) white wine, 2 bay
leaves, salt and freshly ground
black pepper.

1   Preheat the oven to 170°C (150°C
    fan oven) mark 3. Heat the oil in
    a large flameproof casserole and
    lightly brown the lamb shanks
    all over, two or three at a time.
    Remove from the pan and put to
    one side. Add the onion, carrots,
    celery and garlic and cook until
    beginning to colour, then add the
    lamb, tomatoes and wine.
2   Stir well, season and add the bay
    leaves. Bring to the boil, then
    cover and transfer to the oven for
    2 hours or until tender. Skim off
    any fat if necessary.

Braised Lamb Shanks with Cannellini Beans

Hands-on time: 15 minutes
Cooking time: about 2¾ hours

3 tbsp olive oil

6 lamb shanks

1 large onion, chopped

3 carrots, sliced

3 celery sticks, trimmed and sliced

2 garlic cloves, crushed

2 × 400g cans chopped tomatoes

125ml (4fl oz) balsamic vinegar

2 bay leaves

2 × 400g cans cannellini beans, drained and rinsed

salt and freshly ground black pepper

1 Preheat the oven to 170°C (150°C fan oven) mark 3. Heat the oil in a large flameproof casserole and brown the lamb shanks, in two batches, all over. Remove and put to one side.

2 Add the onion, carrots, celery and garlic to the casserole and cook gently until softened and just beginning to colour.

3 Put the lamb back into the casserole, add the tomatoes and vinegar and give the mixture a good stir. Season with salt and ground black pepper and add the bay leaves. Bring to a simmer, cover and cook on the hob for 5 minutes.

4 Transfer to the oven and cook for 1½–2 hours until the lamb shanks are nearly tender.

5 Take the casserole out of the oven and add the cannellini beans. Cover and put back into the oven for a further 30 minutes, then serve.

Serves 6

Braised Lamb Shanks

Hands-on time: about 25 minutes
Cooking time: 2¾ hours

6 small lamb shanks

450g (1lb) whole shallots

2 medium aubergines, cut into
　small dice

2 tbsp olive oil

3 tbsp harissa paste

pared zest of 1 orange and juice of
　3 large oranges

200ml (7fl oz) medium sherry

700g (1½lb) passata

300ml (½ pint) hot lamb or vegetable
　stock (see page 44)

75g (3oz) ready-to-eat dried apricots

75g (3oz) pitted cherries (optional)

a large pinch of saffron threads

couscous and French beans (optional)
　to serve

1　Preheat the oven to 170°C (150°C fan
　oven) mark 3. Heat a large flameproof
　casserole over a medium heat and
　brown the lamb shanks all over. Allow
　10–12 minutes to do this – the better
　the colour now, the better the flavour
　of the finished dish.

2　Remove the lamb and put to one side.
　Add the shallots, aubergines and
　oil to the casserole and cook over a
　high heat, stirring from time to time,
　until the shallots and aubergines are
　golden and beginning to soften.

3　Reduce the heat and add the lamb
　and all the other ingredients except
　the couscous and beans. The liquid
　should come halfway up the shanks.
　Bring to the boil, then cover tightly
　and put into the oven for 2½ hours.
　Test the lamb with a fork – it should
　be so tender that it almost falls off
　the bone.

4　If the cooking liquid looks too thin,
　remove the lamb to a heated serving
　plate, then bubble the sauce on the
　hob until reduced and thickened. Put
　the lamb back into the casserole and
　stir to combine. Serve with couscous,
　and French beans, if you like.

Italian Braised Leg of Lamb

Hands-on time: 15 minutes
Cooking time: about 5 hours

2.3kg (5lb) whole boned leg of lamb, trimmed of fat

50ml (2fl oz) olive oil

700g (1½lb) onions, roughly chopped

1 each red, orange and yellow peppers, seeded and roughly chopped

2 red chillies, seeded and finely chopped (see Safety Tip)

1 garlic bulb, cloves separated and peeled

3 tbsp dried oregano

750ml bottle dry white wine

3 × 400g cans cherry tomatoes

salt and freshly ground black pepper

1 Preheat the oven to 170°C (150°C fan oven) mark 3. Season the lamb with salt and ground black pepper. Heat 2 tbsp of the oil in a large deep flameproof casserole and brown the meat well. Remove and put to one side. Wipe the pan clean.

2 Heat the remaining oil in the casserole and fry the onions, chopped peppers, chillies, garlic and oregano over a medium heat for 10–15 minutes until the onions are translucent and golden brown. Stir in the wine and tomatoes and bring to the boil, then bubble for 10 minutes.

3 Put the lamb on top of the vegetables and season. Baste the meat with the sauce, then cover the casserole tightly with foil and a lid. Cook in the oven for 4 hours, basting occasionally.

4 Uncover and cook for a further 30 minutes. Serve the lamb carved into thick slices with the sauce spooned over.

Serves 6

Braised Beef with Pancetta and Mushrooms

Hands-on time: 20 minutes
Cooking time: about 3½ hours

175g (6oz) smoked pancetta or smoked
  streaky bacon, cubed

2 leeks, trimmed and thickly sliced

1 tbsp olive oil

450g (1lb) braising steak, cut into 5cm
  (2in) pieces

1 large onion, finely chopped

2 carrots, thickly sliced

2 parsnips, thickly sliced

1 tbsp plain flour

300ml (½ pint) red wine

1–2 tbsp redcurrant jelly

125g (4oz) chestnut mushrooms, halved

freshly ground black pepper

freshly chopped flat-leafed parsley
  to garnish

1 Preheat the oven to 170°C (150°C
   fan oven) mark 3. Fry the pancetta
   or bacon in a shallow flameproof
   casserole for 2–3 minutes until golden.
   Add the leeks and cook for a further
   2 minutes or until they are just
   beginning to colour. Remove with a
   slotted spoon and put to one side.

2 Heat the oil in the casserole. Fry the
   beef in batches for 2–3 minutes until
   golden brown on all sides. Remove
   and put to one side. Add the onion and
   fry over a gentle heat for 5 minutes or
   until golden. Stir in the carrots and
   parsnips and fry for 1–2 minutes.

3 Put the beef back into the casserole
   and stir in the flour to soak up the
   juices. Gradually add the wine and
   300ml (½ pint) water, then stir in the
   redcurrant jelly. Season with ground
   black pepper and bring to the boil.
   Cover with a tight-fitting lid and cook
   in the oven for 2 hours.

4 Stir in the leeks, pancetta and
   mushrooms, cover and cook for a
   further 1 hour or until everything
   is tender. Serve hot, sprinkled with
   chopped parsley.

FREEZE AHEAD

To make ahead and freeze, complete the recipe to the end of step 4, without the garnish. Put into a freezerproof container, cool and freeze for up to three months. To use, thaw overnight at cool room temperature. Preheat the oven to 180°C (160°C fan oven) mark 4. Bring the braise to the boil on the hob, then cover tightly and reheat in the oven for about 30 minutes until piping hot.

Serves 4

Braised Beef with Chestnuts and Celery

🍴 **Hands-on time:** 25 minutes
Cooking time: about 2¼ hours

18 fresh chestnuts, skins split

15g (½oz) butter

1 tbsp vegetable oil

2 bacon rashers, rind removed, chopped

900g (2lb) stewing steak, cubed

1 medium onion, chopped

1 tbsp plain flour

300ml (½ pint) brown ale

300ml (½ pint) beef stock

a pinch of freshly grated nutmeg

finely grated zest and juice of 1 orange

3 celery sticks, chopped

salt and freshly ground black pepper

freshly chopped flat-leafed parsley
   to garnish

1 Preheat the oven to 170°C (150°C fan oven) mark 3. Cook the chestnuts in simmering water for about 7 minutes. Remove from the water one at a time and peel off the thick outer skin and thin inner skin while still warm.

2 Heat the butter and oil in a flameproof casserole. Add the bacon and beef in batches and cook, stirring occasionally, until browned. Remove the meat with a slotted spoon.

3 Add the onion to the casserole and fry, stirring, until softened. Drain off most of the fat. Put the meat back into the casserole, sprinkle in the flour and cook, stirring, for 1–2 minutes.

4 Stir in the brown ale, stock, nutmeg, orange juice and half the zest and season to taste. Bring to the boil, then stir well to loosen the sediment and add the chestnuts. Cover tightly with foil and a lid and cook in the oven for about 45 minutes.

5 After 45 minutes, add the celery to the casserole and cook for a further 1 hour or until the meat is tender. Serve with the remaining orange zest and the parsley sprinkled over the top.

Serves 6

Smoky Pimento Goulash

Hands-on time: 20 minutes
Cooking time: about 3 hours

1.1kg (2½lb) braising steak

3 tbsp olive oil, plus extra to drizzle

16 whole shallots or button onions

225g (8oz) piece chorizo sausage,
    roughly chopped

1 red chilli, seeded and chopped
    (see Safety Tip, page 119)

3 bay leaves

3 garlic cloves, crushed

2 tbsp plain flour

2 tbsp smoked paprika

700g jar passata

100ml (3½fl oz) hot beef stock

salt and freshly ground black pepper

mashed potatoes and green vegetables
    to serve

For the minted soured cream

284ml carton soured cream

1 tbsp finely chopped fresh mint

1 tbsp extra virgin olive oil, plus extra
    to drizzle

1 Mix together all the ingredients for the minted soured cream and season with a little salt and plenty of coarsely ground black pepper. Cover and chill in the fridge until needed.

2 Preheat the oven to 170°C (150°C fan oven) mark 3. Cut the braising steak into large cubes, slightly larger than bite-size.

3 Heat the oil in a 4 litre (7 pint) flameproof casserole until really hot. Brown the beef, a few cubes at a time, over a high heat until it is deep brown all over. Remove with a slotted spoon and put to one side. Repeat with the remaining beef until all the pieces have been browned.

4 Reduce the heat under the casserole, then add the shallots or button onions, the chorizo, chilli, bay leaves and garlic. Fry for 7–10 minutes until the shallots are golden brown and beginning to soften. Put the meat back into the casserole and stir in the flour and paprika. Cook, stirring, for

1–2 minutes, then add the passata and season.

5 Cover and cook in the oven for 2½ hours or until the beef is meltingly tender. Check halfway through cooking – if the beef looks dry, add the hot stock. Serve with the minted soured cream, drizzled with a little olive oil and a grinding of black pepper, and some creamy mashed potatoes and green vegetables.

SAVE TIME

Complete the recipe, cool and chill up to three days ahead, or freeze for up to one month. To use, if frozen, thaw overnight at a cool room temperature. Put the goulash back into the casserole, bring to the boil, reduce the heat and simmer gently for 15–20 minutes until piping hot, adding 100ml (3½fl oz) hot beef stock if it looks dry.

Serves 8

Steak and Onion Puff Pie

Hands-on time: 30 minutes
Cooking time: about 2½ hours

3 tbsp vegetable oil

2 onions, sliced

900g (2lb) casserole beef, cut into chunks

3 tbsp plain flour, plus extra to dust

500ml (17fl oz) hot beef stock

2 fresh rosemary sprigs, bruised

500g pack puff pastry

1 medium egg, beaten, to glaze

salt and freshly ground black pepper

1 Preheat the oven to 170°C (150°C fan oven) mark 3.

2 Heat 1 tbsp of the oil in a large flameproof casserole. Add the onions and sauté for 10 minutes or until golden. Lift out and put to one side. Sear the meat in the same casserole, in batches, using more oil as necessary, until brown all over. Lift out each batch as soon as it is browned and put to one side. Add the flour to the casserole and cook for 1–2 minutes to brown. Put the onions and beef back into the casserole, add the hot stock and the rosemary and season well with salt and ground black pepper. Cover and bring to the boil, then cook in the oven for 1½ hours or until the meat is tender.

3 About 30 minutes before the end of the cooking time, lightly dust a worksurface with flour and roll out the pastry. Using a 1.1 litre (2 pint) pie dish as a template, cut out a lid, or use four 300ml (½ pint) dishes and cut out four lids. Put on a baking sheet and chill.

4 Take the casserole out of the oven. Increase the oven temperature to 220°C (200°C fan oven) mark 7. Pour the beef mixture into the pie dish (or dishes), brush the edge with water and put on the pastry lid. Press lightly to seal. Lightly score the top and brush with the egg. Put the dish back on the baking sheet and bake for 30 minutes or until the pastry is risen and golden. Serve immediately.

FREEZE AHEAD

To make ahead and freeze, complete the recipe to the end of step 3. Cool the casserole quickly. Put the beef mixture into a pie dish. Brush the dish edge with water, put on the pastry and press down lightly to seal. Score the pastry. Cover with clingfilm and freeze for up to three months.

To use, thaw overnight at cool room temperature or in the fridge. Lightly score the pastry, brush with beaten egg and cook in an oven preheated to 220°C (200°C fan oven) mark 7 for 35 minutes or until the pastry is brown and the filling piping hot.

Serves 4

Slow-cooker Suppers

Perfect Slow Cooker

A slow cooker is perfect for the cook with a busy lifestyle. We relish the stews and casseroles our grandmothers would have dished up for a midweek supper without a second thought, but now they're a treat for the weekend when we have more time to prepare them. However, a slow cooker solves that problem: switch it on as you leave in the morning and you'll return home at the end of the day to a delicious, home-cooked meal.

What is a slow cooker and how does it work?

A slow cooker is a standalone electrical appliance, designed to be plugged in and left gently cooking unsupervised for hours, without burning or drying up the food. It consists of a lidded round or oval earthenware or ceramic pot that sits in a metal housing containing the heating element, which heats the contents to a steady temperature of around 100°C. Little steam can escape and it condenses in the lid, forming a seal that keeps the temperature constant and the food moist. It also means that a suet pudding can be left to cook for hours without needing to top up the water.

Depending on the model, there are two or three cooking settings (Low, Medium and High) and a Keep Warm function. These settings give you the option to cook a dish on High for just a few hours or on Low all day or overnight. Multi-functional models can also be used as rice cookers and steamers. Older-style slow cookers have a fixed pot to contain the food, but, nowadays, most contain a removable, dishwasher-friendly pot that can be taken straight to the table for serving.

Want to save on washing up? Choose a removable pot that can be used to start off the dish on the hob then transferred to the slow cooker unit. Alternatively, use slow cooker liners (available from specialist websites) if you have a fixed pot slow cooker.

Choosing a slow cooker

Anyone can use a slow cooker: some models are ideal for large families or the cook who likes to stock up the freezer, while smaller versions are suitable for couples or for students living in a bedsit. Otherwise, choose yours according to what you most like to cook: are you only planning to use it for casseroles, will you want to cook a whole chicken, or are you hoping to make plenty of steamed puddings? Make sure you check the size before you buy.

What you can cook in a slow cooker?

Practically anything! Don't just stick to soups, stews and casseroles. You can steam suet puddings (a brilliant hob-space saver at Christmas time), braise joints of meat and whole chickens and even bake cakes and make pâtés. Set it to cook overnight and you can enjoy a bowl of warming porridge for breakfast too. Cooking food in a slow cooker has many benefits: flavours have time to develop and even the toughest of cuts of meat become incredibly tender. It's important to raise the temperature quickly to destroy harmful bacteria, so, either bring the food to boiling point on the hob first or preheat the slow cooker – always follow the manufacturer's instructions.

What you can't cook in a slow cooker?

Not much! But obviously very large joints of meat and poultry such as turkey aren't suitable, while roasts and stir-fries are out of the question. Some foods, such as pasta, rice, fish, puddings and cakes, are only suitable for shorter slow cooking times, so always check the recipe. Milk and cream will separate if cooked for a long time – add them to finish off and enrich a dish in the last few minutes or so of cooking time. Always fully immerse potatoes to stop them blackening while cooking.

Saving money with a slow cooker

Not only are slow cookers practical, they're also economical, because:

- Tougher cuts of meat, such as oxtail, shin of beef or lamb shanks, tend to be cheaper and benefit from long, slow cooking at low temperatures. Perfect for the slow cooker
- They use far less energy than a conventional oven because you are only heating up a small piece of equipment that runs on a minute amount of power in comparison
- They're ideal for flexible meal times, saving you cash and conserving energy. A slow cooker is especially useful for large active families who eat at different times – prepare one dish, then keep it warm in the pot for up to two hours

Slow cooker safety tips

- Always stand the appliance on a heat-resistant surface
- Do not use a slow cooker to reheat cold or frozen food – the temperature rises too slowly to kill harmful bacteria. Heat first on the hob, then transfer to the slow cooker pot
- Always use oven gloves to remove the pot from the slow cooker
- Never immerse the outer housing in water; stand it on a draining board to clean and remove the flex if possible
- Never fill the outer housing with food; always use the inner pot
- Don't let young children touch the slow cooker – the housing and the lid can become very hot or spit boiling water
- Be careful when cooking with dried beans – for example, kidney beans need to be boiled vigorously for 10 minutes to remove harmful toxins. Do this in a pan on the hob before draining and continuing with the recipe in the slow cooker

Mexican Bean Soup

Hands-on time: 15 minutes
Cooking time: 10 minutes in pan, then about 3 hours on High, plus cooling

4 tbsp olive oil

1 onion, chopped

2 garlic cloves, chopped

a pinch of crushed dried red chillies

1 tsp ground coriander

1 tsp ground cumin

½ tsp ground cinnamon

600ml (1 pint) hot vegetable stock

300ml (½ pint) tomato juice

1–2 tsp chilli sauce

2 × 400g cans red kidney beans, drained
   and rinsed

2 tbsp freshly chopped coriander

salt and freshly ground black pepper

fresh coriander leaves, roughly torn,
   to garnish

crusty bread and lime butter to serve
   (optional, see below)

Lime Butter

Beat the grated zest and juice of
½ lime into 50g (2oz) softened butter
and season to taste. Shape into a log,
wrap in clingfilm and chill until needed.
To serve, unwrap and slice thinly.

1 Heat the oil in a large pan, add the
   onion, garlic, chillies and spices
   and fry gently for 5 minutes or until
   lightly golden.

2 Add the hot stock, the tomato juice,
   chilli sauce and beans and bring to
   the boil, then transfer to the slow
   cooker, cover and cook on High for
   2–3 hours.

3 Leave the soup to cool a little, then
   whiz in batches in a blender or food
   processor until very smooth. Pour
   the soup into a clean pan, stir in the
   chopped coriander and heat through
   gently on the hob – do not boil.
   Season to taste with salt and ground
   black pepper.

4 Ladle the soup into warmed bowls.
   Top each portion with a few slices of
   lime butter, if you like, and scatter
   with torn coriander leaves.

Scotch Broth

Hands-on time: 15 minutes
Cooking time: 20 minutes in pan, then about 10 hours on Low

1.4kg (3lb) piece beef skirt (ask your butcher for this)

300g (11oz) broth mix (to include pearl barley, red lentils, split peas and green peas), soaked according to the pack instructions

2 carrots, finely chopped

1 parsnip, finely chopped

2 onions, finely chopped

¼ white cabbage, finely chopped

1 leek, trimmed and finely chopped

1 piece marrow bone (weight about 350g/12oz)

½ tbsp salt

freshly ground black pepper

2 tbsp freshly chopped parsley and crusty bread to serve

1 Put the beef into a large pan and cover with water. Slowly bring to the boil, then reduce the heat and simmer for 10 minutes, using a slotted spoon to remove any scum that comes to the surface. Drain.

2 Put the broth mix and all the vegetables into the slow cooker, then place the beef and marrow bone on top. Add 1.5 litres (2½ pints) boiling water – there should be enough to just cover the meat. Cover and cook on Low for 8–10 hours until the meat is tender.

3 Remove the marrow bone and beef from the broth. Add a few shreds of beef to the broth, if you like. Season the broth well with the salt and some ground black pepper, then stir in the chopped parsley and serve hot with crusty bread.

SAVE EFFORT

This can be two meals in one: a starter and a main course. The beef flavours the stock and is removed before serving. You can then divide up the meat and serve it with mashed potatoes, swedes or turnips.

Serves 8

Easy Chicken Casserole

Hands-on time: 15 minutes
Cooking time: 10 minutes in pan, then about 6 hours on Low

1 tbsp sunflower oil

1 small chicken, weight about 1.4kg (3lb)

1 fresh rosemary sprig

2 bay leaves

1 red onion, cut into wedges

2 carrots, cut into chunks

2 leeks, trimmed and cut into chunks

2 celery sticks, cut into chunks

12 baby new potatoes, halved if large

900ml (1½ pints) hot chicken stock

200g (7oz) green beans, trimmed

salt and freshly ground black pepper

1 Heat the oil in a large pan over a medium heat. Add the chicken and fry until browned all over. Put the chicken into the slow cooker, along with the herbs and all the vegetables except the green beans. Season well.

2 Pour in the hot stock, cover and cook on Low for 5–6 hours until the chicken is cooked through. Add the beans for the last hour or cook separately in lightly salted boiling water and stir into the casserole once it's cooked. To test the chicken is cooked, pierce the thickest part of the leg with a knife: the juices should run clear.

3 Remove the chicken and spoon the vegetables into six bowls. Carve the chicken and divide among the bowls, then ladle the cooking liquid over.

SAVE EFFORT

For a different serving suggestion, omit the baby new potatoes and serve with mashed potatoes.

Serves 6

Spanish Chicken

Slow Cooker Recipe

Hands-on time: 25 minutes, plus infusing
Cooking time: about 20 minutes in pan, then about 2 hours on Low

1 tsp ground turmeric

1.1 litres (2 pints) hot chicken stock

2 tbsp vegetable oil

4 boneless, skinless chicken thighs, roughly diced

1 onion, chopped

1 red pepper, seeded and sliced

50g (2oz) chorizo sausage, diced

2 garlic cloves, crushed

300g (11oz) long-grain rice

125g (4oz) frozen peas

salt and freshly ground black pepper

3 tbsp freshly chopped flat-leafed parsley to garnish

crusty bread to serve

1 Add the turmeric to the hot stock and leave to infuse for at least 5 minutes. Meanwhile, heat the oil in a large frying pan over a medium heat. Add the chicken and fry for 10 minutes or until golden, then transfer to the slow cooker.

2 Add the onion to the pan and cook over a medium heat for 5 minutes or until soft. Add the red pepper and chorizo and cook for a further 5 minutes, then add the garlic and cook for 1 minute.

3 Add the rice and mix well. Pour in the stock and peas and season, then transfer to the slow cooker and stir together. Cover and cook on Low for 1–2 hours until the rice is tender and the chicken is cooked through.

4 Check the seasoning and garnish with the parsley. Serve with some crusty bread.

Serves 4

Chicken Tagine with Apricots and Almonds

Hands-on time: 10 minutes
Cooking time: about 15 minutes in pan, then about 5 hours on Low

2 tbsp olive oil

4 chicken thighs

1 onion, chopped

2 tsp ground cinnamon

2 tbsp runny honey

150g (5oz) dried apricots

75g (3oz) blanched almonds

125ml (4fl oz) hot chicken stock

salt and freshly ground black pepper

flaked almonds to garnish

couscous to serve

1. Heat 1 tbsp of the oil in a large pan over a medium heat. Add the chicken and fry for 5 minutes or until brown, then transfer to the slow cooker.

2. Add the onion to the pan with the remaining oil and fry for 10 minutes or until softened.

3. Add the cinnamon, honey, apricots, almonds and hot stock to the onion and season well. Bring to the boil, then transfer to the slow cooker, cover and cook on Low for 4–5 hours until the chicken is tender and cooked through. Garnish with the flaked almonds and serve hot with couscous.

Serves 4

Chicken with Chorizo and Beans

Hands-on time: 10 minutes
Cooking time: about 20 minutes in pan, then about 5 hours on Low

Slow Cooker Recipe

1 tbsp olive oil

12 chicken pieces (6 drumsticks and 6 thighs)

175g (6oz) chorizo sausage, cubed

1 onion, finely chopped

2 large garlic cloves, crushed

1 tsp mild chilli powder

3 red peppers, seeded and roughly chopped

400g (14oz) passata

2 tbsp tomato purée

150ml (¼ pint) hot chicken stock

2 × 400g cans butter beans, drained and rinsed

200g (7oz) new potatoes, quartered

1 small bunch of fresh thyme

1 bay leaf

200g (7oz) baby leaf spinach

SAVE EFFORT

An easy way to get a brand new dish is to use mixed beans instead of butter beans.

1 Heat the oil in a large pan over a medium heat. Add the chicken and fry until browned all over, then transfer to the slow cooker.

2 Add the chorizo to the pan and fry for 2–3 minutes until its oil starts to run. Add the onion, garlic and chilli powder and fry over a low heat for 5 minutes or until the onion is soft.

3 Add the red peppers and cook for 2–3 minutes until soft. Stir in the passata, tomato purée, hot stock, butter beans, potatoes, thyme sprigs and bay leaf. Bring to the boil, then add to the chicken. Cover and cook on Low for 4–5 hours until the chicken is cooked through.

4 Remove the thyme and bay leaf, then stir in the spinach until it wilts. Serve immediately.

Serves 6

Mexican Chilli Con Carne

Slow Cooker Recipe

🍴 **Hands-on time:** 5 minutes
Cooking time: 25 minutes in pan, then about 5 hours on Low

2 tbsp olive oil

450g (1lb) minced beef

1 large onion, finely chopped

½–1 tsp hot chilli powder

½–1 tsp ground cumin

3 tbsp tomato purée

150ml (¼ pint) hot beef stock

400g can chopped tomatoes with garlic
(see Save Time)

25g (1oz) dark chocolate

400g can red kidney beans, drained
and rinsed

2 × 20g packs of fresh coriander,
chopped

salt and freshly ground black pepper

guacamole, salsa, soured cream, grated
cheese, tortilla chips and pickled
chillies to serve

SAVE TIME

If you can't find a can of tomatoes
with garlic, use a can of chopped
tomatoes and 1 crushed garlic clove.

1 Heat 1 tbsp of the oil in a large pan
and fry the beef for 10 minutes or until
well browned, stirring to break up any
lumps. Remove from the pan with a
slotted spoon and transfer to the
slow cooker.

2 Add the remaining oil to the pan, then
fry the onion, stirring, for 10 minutes
or until soft and golden.

3 Add the spices and fry for 1 minute,
then add the tomato purée, hot stock
and the tomatoes. Bring to the boil,
then stir into the mince in the slow
cooker. Cover and cook on Low for
4–5 hours.

4 Stir in the chocolate, kidney beans
and coriander and season with salt
and ground black pepper, then leave
to stand for 10 minutes.

5 Serve with guacamole, salsa, soured
cream, grated cheese, tortilla chips
and pickled chillies.

Serves 4

Beef Goulash

Hands-on time: 30 minutes
Cooking time: about 20 minutes in pan, then about 10 hours on Low

2 tbsp plain flour

1kg (2¼lb) stewing steak, cut into 3cm (1¼in) cubes

3 tbsp vegetable oil

700g (1½lb) onions, chopped

225g (8oz) pancetta cubes or bacon lardons

2 garlic cloves, crushed

4 tbsp paprika

2 tsp dried mixed herbs

400g can peeled plum tomatoes

150ml (¼ pint) hot beef stock

150ml (¼ pint) soured cream

salt and freshly ground black pepper

freshly chopped parsley to garnish

noodles to serve

1 Put the flour into a plastic bag, season with salt and ground black pepper, then toss the cubes of beef in the flour to coat and shake off any excess.

2 Heat 2 tbsp of the oil in a large pan and quickly fry the meat in small batches until browned on all sides. Transfer to the slow cooker.

3 Heat the remaining oil in the pan, add the onions and fry gently for 5–7 minutes until starting to soften and turn golden. Add the pancetta or lardons and fry over a high heat until crispy. Stir in the garlic and paprika and cook, stirring, for 1 minute.

4 Add the herbs, tomatoes and hot stock and bring to the boil. Stir into the beef in the slow cooker, then cover and cook on Low for 8–10 hours until tender.

5 Check the seasoning, then stir in the soured cream. Garnish with parsley and serve with noodles.

Serves 6

Beef and Stout Stew

Slow Cooker Recipe

Hands-on time: 15 minutes
Cooking time: 25 minutes in pan, then about 10 hours on Low

2 tbsp plain flour

1.4kg (3lb) shin of beef or braising steak, cut into 3cm (1¼in) cubes

4 tbsp vegetable oil

2 medium onions, sliced

4 medium carrots, cut into chunks

225ml (8fl oz) Guinness

300ml (½ pint) hot beef stock

2 bay leaves

700g (1½lb) baby potatoes, halved if large

2 tbsp freshly chopped flat-leafed parsley

salt and freshly ground black pepper

mashed potatoes, mangetout and peas to serve

1 Put the flour into a plastic bag, season with salt and ground black pepper, then toss the beef in the flour to coat and shake off any excess. Heat the oil in a large pan until hot. Add a handful of beef and cook until well browned. Remove with a slotted spoon and transfer to the slow cooker, then repeat until all the meat is browned.

2 Add the onions and carrots to the pan and cook for 10 minutes or until browned. Add the Guinness, scraping the bottom of the pan to loosen the goodness, then stir in the hot stock. Add the bay leaves and potatoes and bring to the boil. Pour over the beef in the slow cooker, cover and cook on Low for 8–10 hours until the meat is tender.

3 Stir in the chopped parsley, season to taste with salt and ground black pepper and serve.

Serves 6

Pheasant Casserole with Cider and Apples

Slow Cooker Recipe

Hands-on time: 50 minutes
Cooking time: about 25 minutes in pan, then about 7 hours on Low

2 large oven-ready pheasants

2 tbsp plain flour, plus extra to dust

50g (2oz) butter

4 rindless streaky bacon rashers, halved

2 onions, chopped

2 celery sticks, chopped

1 tbsp dried juniper berries,
    lightly crushed

2.5cm (1in) piece fresh root ginger,
    peeled and finely chopped

150ml (¼ pint) hot pheasant or chicken
    stock (see page 44)

350ml (12fl oz) dry cider

150ml (¼ pint) double cream

4 crisp eating apples, such as
    Granny Smith

1 tbsp lemon juice

salt and freshly ground black pepper

1 Cut each pheasant into four portions, season with salt and ground black pepper and dust with flour.

2 Melt three-quarters of the butter in a large pan and brown the pheasant portions, in batches, over a high heat until deep golden brown on all sides. Transfer to the slow cooker.

3 Add the bacon to the pan and fry for 2–3 minutes until golden. Add the onions, celery, juniper berries and ginger and cook for 8–10 minutes.

4 Stir in the flour and cook, stirring, for 2 minutes, then add the hot stock and the cider and bring to the boil, stirring. Pour into the slow cooker and season well, then cover and cook on Low for 6–7 hours until the pheasant is tender.

5 Lift out the pheasant and put into a warmed dish and keep it warm. Strain the sauce through a sieve into a pan. Stir in the cream, bring to the boil and bubble for 10 minutes or until syrupy.

6 Quarter, core and cut the apples into wedges, then toss in the lemon juice. Melt the remaining butter in a small pan and fry the apple wedges for 2–3 minutes until golden. Put the pheasant back into the sauce, along with the apples, and check the seasoning before serving.

Serves 8

Curried Lamb with Lentils

Hands-on time: 15 minutes, plus marinating
Cooking time: 20 minutes in pan, then about 6 hours on Low

500g (1lb 2oz) lean stewing lamb on the bone, cut into 8 pieces (ask your butcher to do this), trimmed of fat

1 tsp ground cumin

1 tsp ground turmeric

2 garlic cloves, crushed

1 medium red chilli, seeded and chopped (see Safety Tip, page 119)

2.5cm (1in) piece fresh root ginger, peeled and grated

2 tbsp vegetable oil

1 onion, chopped

400g can chopped tomatoes

2 tbsp vinegar

175g (6oz) red lentils, rinsed

salt and freshly ground black pepper

fresh coriander sprigs to garnish

rocket salad to serve

1 Put the lamb into a shallow sealable container and add the spices, garlic, chilli, ginger, salt and ground black pepper. Stir well to mix, then cover and chill for at least 30 minutes.

2 Heat the oil in a large pan, add the onion and cook over a low heat for 5 minutes. Add the lamb and cook for 10 minutes, turning regularly, or until the meat is evenly browned.

3 Add the tomatoes, vinegar, lentils and 225ml (8fl oz) boiling water and bring to the boil. Season well. Transfer to the slow cooker, cover and cook on Low for 5–6 hours until the lamb is tender.

4 Serve hot, garnished with coriander, with a rocket salad.

Serves 4

Delicious Puddings
and Desserts

Chocolate and Hazelnut Meringues

Hands-on time: 25 minutes, plus softening
Cooking time: 2 hours 10 minutes, plus cooling

125g (4oz) hazelnuts

125g (4oz) caster sugar

75g (3oz) plain chocolate (at least 70% cocoa solids)

2 medium egg whites

300ml (½ pint) double cream

redcurrants, blackberries and chocolate shavings to decorate

Caramel-dipped Physalis (Cape gooseberries) to serve (see opposite, optional)

1 Preheat the oven to 110°C (90°C fan oven) mark ¼ and preheat the grill. Line two baking sheets with non-stick baking parchment. Spread the hazelnuts over a baking sheet and toast under the hot grill until golden brown, turning them frequently. Put the hazelnuts into a clean teatowel and rub off the skins, then put the nuts into a food processor with 3 tbsp of the sugar and process to a fine powder. Add the chocolate and pulse until roughly chopped.

2 Put the egg whites into a clean grease-free bowl and whisk until stiff. Whisk in the remaining sugar, a spoonful at a time, until the mixture is stiff and shiny. Fold in the nut mixture.

3 Spoon the mixture on to the prepared baking sheets, making small rough mounds about 9cm (3½in) in diameter. Bake for about 45 minutes until the meringues will just peel off the paper. Gently push in the base of each meringue to form a deep hollow, then put back into the oven for 1¼ hours or until crisp and dry. Leave to cool.

4 Whip the cream until it just holds its shape, then spoon three-quarters on to the meringues. Leave in the fridge to soften for up to 2 hours.

5 Decorate the meringues with the remaining cream, the fruit and chocolate shavings. Serve immediately, with Caramel-dipped Physalis, if you like.

Caramel-dipped Physalis

To make the caramel, dissolve 125g (4oz) caster sugar in a small heavy-based pan over a low heat. Bring to the boil and bubble until a golden caramel colour. Holding each physalis by the papery leaves, dip it into the caramel, then place on an oiled baking sheet and leave to cool.

SAVE TIME

Complete the recipe to the end of step 3, then store the meringues in an airtight container up to one week ahead. Complete steps 4 and 5 to finish the recipe.

Serves 6

Orange and Chocolate Cheesecake

Hands-on time: 45 minutes
Cooking time: about 2¼ hours, plus cooling

225g (8oz) chilled unsalted butter, plus extra to grease

250g (9oz) plain flour, sifted

150g (5oz) light muscovado sugar

3 tbsp cocoa powder

chocolate curls to decorate (see opposite)

For the topping

2 oranges

800g (1¾lb) cream cheese

250g (9oz) mascarpone

4 large eggs

225g (8oz) golden caster sugar

2 tbsp cornflour

½ tsp vanilla extract

1 vanilla pod

1 Preheat the oven to 180°C (160°C fan oven) mark 4. Grease a 23cm (9in) springform cake tin and base-line with baking parchment.

2 Cut 175g (6oz) of the butter into cubes. Melt the remaining butter and put to one side. Put the flour and cubed butter into a food processor with the muscovado sugar and cocoa powder and whiz until the texture of fine breadcrumbs. (Alternatively, rub the butter into the flour in a large bowl by hand or using a pastry blender. Stir in the sugar and cocoa.) Pour in the melted butter and pulse, or stir with a fork, until the mixture comes together.

3 Spoon the crumb mixture into the prepared tin and press evenly on to the bottom, using the back of a metal spoon to level the surface. Bake for 35–40 minutes until lightly puffed; avoid overbrowning or the biscuit base will have a bitter flavour. Take out of the oven and leave to cool. Reduce the oven temperature to 150°C (130°C fan oven) mark 2.

4 Meanwhile, make the topping. Grate the zest from the oranges, then squeeze the juice – you will need 150ml (¼ pint). Put the cream cheese, mascarpone, eggs, sugar, cornflour, grated orange zest and vanilla extract

into a large bowl. Using a hand-held electric whisk, beat the ingredients together thoroughly until combined.

5 Split the vanilla pod in half lengthways and, using the tip of a sharp knife, scrape out the seeds and add them to the cheese mixture. Beat in the orange juice and continue whisking until the mixture is smooth.

6 Pour the cheese mixture over the cooled biscuit base. Bake for about 1½ hours until pale golden on top, slightly risen and just set around the edge. The cheesecake should still be slightly wobbly in the middle; it will set as it cools. Turn off the oven and leave the

cheesecake inside, with the door ajar, to cool for 1 hour. Remove and leave to cool completely (about 3 hours), then chill in the fridge.

7 Just before serving, unclip the tin and transfer the cheesecake to a plate. Scatter chocolate curls on top to decorate, if you like.

Chocolate Curls

Melt some chocolate, then spread it out in a thin layer on a marble slab or clean worksurface. Leave to firm up. Using a sharp, flat-ended blade, scrape through the chocolate at a 45-degree angle.

Serves 4

Fruity Rice Pudding

Hands-on time: 10 minutes
Cooking time: about 3 hours on Low, plus cooling and chilling (optional)

125g (4oz) short-grain pudding rice

1.1 litres (2 pints) full-fat milk

1 tsp vanilla extract

3–4 tbsp caster sugar

200ml (7fl oz) whipping cream

6 tbsp wild lingonberry sauce

1 Put the rice into the slow cooker with the milk, vanilla and sugar. Cover and cook on Low for 2–3 hours. You can enjoy the pudding hot now or leave it to cool and continue the recipe.
2 Lightly whip the cream and fold through the pudding. Chill for 1 hour.
3 Divide the rice mixture among six glass dishes and top each with 1 tbsp lingonberry sauce.

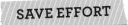

WITHOUT A SLOW COOKER

Put the rice into a pan with 600ml (1 pint) cold water. Bring to the boil, then reduce the heat and simmer until the liquid has evaporated. Add the milk, bring to the boil, then reduce the heat and simmer for 45 minutes or until soft and creamy. Leave to cool, then complete steps 2 and 3 to finish the recipe.

SAVE EFFORT

For an alternative presentation, serve in tumblers, layering the rice pudding with the fruit sauce; you will need to use double the amount of fruit sauce.

Serves 6

Winter Fruit Compote

Slow Cooker Recipe

🍴 **Hands-on time:** 10 minutes
Cooking time: 5 minutes in pan, then about 4 hours on Low

75g (3oz) readyto-eat dried pears
75g (3oz) ready-to-eat dried figs
75g (3oz) ready-to-eat dried apricots
75g (3oz) ready-to-eat prunes
1 star anise
½ cinnamon stick
300ml (½ pint) apple juice
300ml (½ pint) dry white wine
light muscovado sugar to taste (optional)
crème fraîche or thick Greek yogurt to serve

1 Put the dried fruits into the slow cooker with the star anise and cinnamon stick.
2 Pour the apple juice and wine into a pan and bring to the boil. Pour over the fruit, cover and cook on Low for 3–4 hours until plump and tender.
3 Sprinkle the sugar over the fruit if you like, and serve the compote with crème fraîche or thick Greek yogurt.

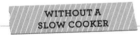

WITHOUT A SLOW COOKER

Put the dried fruits, spices, apple juice and wine into a pan and bring to the boil slowly. Reduce the heat, cover and simmer for 45 minutes or until the fruits are plump and tender. Top up the liquid if necessary. Complete step 3 to finish the recipe.

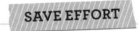

SAVE EFFORT

For an easy way to get a brand new dish, replace the figs with dried apple rings and the pears with raisins.

Serves 6

Cranberry Christmas Pudding

Hands-on time: 20 minutes, plus soaking
Cooking time: 8½ hours

200g (7oz) currants

200g (7oz) sultanas

200g (7oz) raisins

75g (3oz) dried cranberries or cherries

grated zest and juice of 1 orange

50ml (2fl oz) rum

50ml (2fl oz) brandy

1–2 tsp Angostura bitters

1 small apple

1 carrot

175g (6oz) fresh breadcrumbs

100g (3½oz) plain flour, sifted

1 tsp mixed spice

175g (6oz) light vegetarian suet

100g (3½oz) dark muscovado sugar

50g (2oz) blanched almonds,
   roughly chopped

2 medium eggs

butter to grease

fresh or frozen cranberries (thawed if
   frozen), fresh bay leaves and icing
   sugar to decorate

Brandy Butter to serve (see opposite)

1 Put the dried fruit, orange zest and juice into a large bowl. Pour the rum, brandy and Angostura bitters over. Cover and leave to soak in a cool place for at least 1 hour or overnight.

2 Peel and grate the apple and carrot and add to the bowl of soaked fruit with the breadcrumbs, flour, mixed spice, suet, sugar, almonds and eggs. Using a wooden spoon, mix everything together well. Grease a 1.8 litre (3¼ pint) pudding basin and line with a 60cm (24in) square piece of muslin. Spoon the mixture into the basin and flatten the surface. Gather the muslin up and over the top, twist and secure with string. Put the basin on an upturned heatproof saucer or trivet in the bottom of a large pan, then pour in enough boiling water to come halfway up the side of the basin. Cover the pan with a tight-fitting lid, bring the water to the boil, then turn down the heat and simmer gently for 6 hours. Top up with more boiling water as necessary.

3 Remove the basin from the pan and leave to cool. When the pudding is cold, remove from the basin, then wrap it in clingfilm and a double layer of foil. Store in a cool, dry place for up to six months.

4 To reheat, steam for 2½ hours; check the water level every 40 minutes and top up with boiling water if necessary. Leave the pudding in the pan, covered, to keep warm until needed.

Decorate with cranberries and bay leaves, dust with icing sugar and serve with Brandy Butter.

Brandy Butter

Put 125g (4oz) unsalted butter into a bowl and beat until very soft. Gradually beat in 125g (4oz) sieved light muscovado sugar until very light and fluffy, then beat in 6 tbsp brandy, a spoonful at a time. Cover and chill for at least 3 hours.

Serves 12

Rich Fruit Cake

Hands-on time: 30 minutes
Cooking time: about 2½ hours, plus cooling

175g (6oz) unsalted butter, cubed, plus extra to grease

1kg (2¼lb) mixed dried fruit

100g (3½oz) ready-to-eat dried prunes, roughly chopped

50g (2oz) ready-to-eat dried figs, roughly chopped

100g (3½oz) dried cranberries

2 balls preserved stem ginger in syrup, grated and syrup reserved

grated zest and juice of 1 orange

175ml (6fl oz) brandy

2 splashes Angostura bitters

175g (6oz) dark muscovado sugar

200g (7oz) self-raising flour

½ tsp ground cinnamon

½ tsp freshly grated nutmeg

½ tsp ground cloves

4 medium eggs, beaten

1 Preheat the oven to 150°C (130°C fan oven) mark 2. Grease a 20.5cm (8in) round deep cake tin and line the base and sides with greaseproof paper.

2 Put all the dried fruit into a very large pan and add the ginger, 1 tbsp reserved ginger syrup, the orange zest and juice, brandy and Angostura bitters. Bring to the boil, then reduce the heat and simmer for 5 minutes. Add the butter and sugar and heat gently to melt. Stir occasionally until the sugar dissolves. Take the pan off the heat and leave to cool for a couple of minutes.

3 Add the flour, spices and beaten eggs and mix well. Pour the mixture into the prepared tin and level the surface. Wrap the outside of the tin in brown paper and secure with string to protect the cake during cooking. Bake for 2–2½ hours – cover with greaseproof paper after about 1½ hours – until the cake is firm to the touch and a skewer inserted into the centre comes out clean.

4 Cool in the tin for 2–3 hours, then remove from the tin, leaving the greaseproof paper on, transfer to a wire rack and leave to cool completely. Wrap the cake in a layer of clingfilm, then in foil.

SAVE TIME

Complete the recipe, then store in an airtight container for up to three months. If you like, after the cake has matured for two weeks, unwrap it and prick it all over with a metal skewer and sprinkle with 1 tbsp brandy. Leave to soak in, then rewrap and store as before.

Cuts into 16 slices

Calorie Gallery

140 cal ♥ 1g protein
11g fat (7g sat) ♥ 2g fibre
10g carb ♥ 0.2g salt
8

290 cal ♥ 3g protein
25g fat (4g sat) ♥ 3g fibre
15g carb 0.2g salt
10

438 cal ♥ 11g protein
21g fat (13g sat) ♥ 4g fibre
45g carb ♥ 1.3g salt
12

117 cal ♥ 3g protein
6g fat (4g sat) ♥ 4g fibre
13g carb ♥ 0.1g salt
14

280 cal ♥ 10g protein
10g fat (1g sat) ♥ 7g fibre
34g carb ♥ 1.3g salt
26

296 cal ♥ 20g protein
5g fat (1g sat) ♥ 9g fibre
47g carb ♥ 0.1g salt
28

262 cal ♥ 7g protein
7g fat (1g sat) ♥ 8g fibre
44g carb ♥ 1.3g salt
30

Per 125g (4oz) serving
(with stuffing): 301 cal
21g protein ♥ 19g fat (9g sat)
1g fibre ♥ 12g carb ♥ 0.9g salt
50

Per 125g (4oz) serving:
286 cal ♥ 21g protein
11g fat (5g sat) ♥ 1g fibre
28g carb ♥ 0.6g salt
54

620 cal ♥ 62g protein
21g fat (6g sat) ♥ 4g fibre
24g carb ♥ 1.7g salt
66

For 8: 550 cal ♥ 55g protein
19g fat (6g sat) ♥ 2g fibre
48g carb ♥ 5.5g salt
For 10: 440 cal ♥ 44g protein
15g fat (5g sat) ♥ 2g fibre
38g carb ♥ 4.4g salt
80

406 cals ♥ 49g protein
21g fat (7g sat) ♥ 0.3g
fibre ♥ 4g carb ♥ 6.3g salt
82

592 cal ♥ 54g protein
18g fat (7g sat) ♥ 2g fibre
56g carb ♥ 1g salt
84

645 cal ♥ 54g protein
51g fat (18g sat) ♥ 0g fibre
0g carb ♥ 0.5g salt
88

400 cal ♥ 27g protein
10g fat (5g sat) ♥ 6g fibre
53g carb ♥ 1.5g salt
16

80 cal ♥ 0.5g protein
7g fat (5g sat) ♥ 0.9 g fibre
3g carb ♥ 0.1g salt
20

50 cal ♥ 0.6g protein
trace fat ♥ 1g fibre
11g carb ♥ 0g salt
22

150 cal ♥ 4g protein
9g fat (1g sat) ♥ 4g fibre
15g carb ♥ 0.1g salt
24

506 cal ♥ 30g protein
28g fat (9g sat) ♥ 1g fibre
10g carb ♥ 1g salt
38

740 cal ♥ 49g protein
44g fat (17g sat) ♥ 3g fibre
26g carb ♥ 1.8g salt
40

854 cal ♥ 58g protein
45g fat (14g sat) ♥ 5g fibre
55g carb ♥ 3g salt

332 cal ♥ 29g protein
21g fat (6g sat) ♥ 0.8g fibre
6g carb ♥ 1.3g salt
42

46

646 cal ♥ 45g protein
41g fat (12g sat) ♥ 2g fibre
11g carb ♥ 1g salt
68

650 cal ♥ 25g protein
33g fat (13g sat) ♥ 2g fibre
65g carb ♥ 1.1g salt
72

617 cals ♥ 31g protein
37g fat (14g sats) 2g fibre
45g carbs ♥ 2g salt
74

348 cal ♥ 28g protein
14g fat (3g sat) ♥ 8g fibre
27g carb ♥ 1.5g salt
76

662 cal ♥ 62g protein
41g fat (19g sat) ♥ 0.2g fibre
3g carb 1.4g salt
92

490 cal ♥ 39g protein
22g fat (9g sat) ♥ 2g fibre
32g carb ♥ 0.8g salt
94

536 cal ♥ 51g protein
28g fat (12g sat) ♥ 2g fibre
14g carb ♥ 1.2g salt
96

530 cal ♥ 30g protein
33g fat (20g sat) ♥ 4g fibre
27g carb ♥ 0.5g salt
98

419 cal ♥ 46g protein
20g fat (9g sat) ♥ 3g fibre
24g carb ♥ 0.6g salt

100

616 cal ♥ 56g protein
35g fat (12g sat) ♥ 5g fibre
16g carb ♥ 1.2g salt

102

540 cal ♥ 35g protein
24g fat (7g sat) ♥ 5g fibre
24g carb ♥ 1.5g salt

104

807 cals ♥ 59g protein
53g fat (24g sats) ♥ 0g fibre
2g carbs ♥ 0.5g salt

108

541 cal ♥ 34g protein
25g fat (9g sat) ♥ 6g fibre
30g carb ♥ 1.6g salt

120

336 cal ♥ 35g protein
16g fat (6g sat) ♥ 2g fibre
12g carb ♥ 1.3g salt

122

515 cal ♥ 36g protein
35g fat (14g sat) ♥ 1g fibre
13g carb ♥ 1.3g salt

124

671 cal ♥ 23g protein
28g fat (5g sat) ♥ 3g fibre
70g carb ♥ 0.8g salt

140

376 cal ♥ 18g protein
22g fat (4g sat) ♥ 4g fibre
19g carb ♥ 0.5g salt

142

690 cal ♥ 35g protein
41g fat (12g sat) ♥ 8g fibre
33g carb ♥ 2.6g salt

144

478 cal ♥ 45g protein
22g fat (7g sat) ♥ 3g fibre
36g carb ♥ 0.3g salt

154

520 cal ♥ 5g protein
42g fat (19g sat) ♥ 2g fibre
32g carb ♥ 0.1g salt

158

767 cal ♥ 8g protein
60g fat (37g sat) ♥ 0.8g fibre
53g carb ♥ 1.2g salt

160

323 cal ♥ 7g protein
17g fat (10g sat) ♥ 0.1g fibre
36g carb ♥ 0.2g salt

162

322 cal ♥ 57g protein
8g fat (3g sat) ♥ 0g fibre
4g carb ♥ 0.5g salt

110

382 cal ♥ 37g protein
18g fat (6g sat) ♥ 9g fibre
29g carb ♥ 1.2g salt

114

355 cal ♥ 30g protein
16g fat (6g sat) ♥ 4g fibre
23g carb ♥ 1.2g salt

116

474 cal ♥ 39g protein
27g fat (11g sat) ♥ 2g fibre
11g carb ♥ 0.7g salt

118

1036 cal ♥ 55g protein
67g fat (10g sat) ♥ 1g fibre
65g carb ♥ 1.4g salt

126

Without lime butter: 184 cal
4g protein ♥ 8g fat (1g sat)
4g fibre ♥ 21g carb ♥ 1.3g salt

134

173 cal ♥ 8g protein
2g fat (trace fat) ♥ 4g fibre
35g carb ♥ 2.3g salt

136

323 cal ♥ 31g protein
18g fat (5g sat) ♥ 3g fibre
17g carb ♥ 0.9g salt

138

408 cal ♥ 29g protein
19g fat (7g sat) ♥ 0g fibre
28g carb ♥ 1.1g salt

146

517 cal ♥ 46g protein
30g fat (116 sat) ♥ 2g fibre
16g carb ♥ 1.6g salt

148

586 cal ♥ 52g protein
29g fat (10g sat) ♥ 3g fibre
31 carb ♥ 0.4g salt

150

478 cal ♥ 32g protein
28g fat (16g sat) ♥ 2g fibre
12g carb ♥ 0.7g salt

152

139 cal ♥ 1g protein
trace fat ♥ 3g fibre
26g carb ♥ 0.1g salt

164

448 cal ♥ 5g protein
17g fat (7g sat) ♥ 2g fibre
68g carb ♥ 0.3g salt

166

Per slice: 384 cal
5g protein ♥ 11g fat (6g sat)
2g fibre ♥ 71g carb ♥ 0.2g salt

168

Index

PICTURE CREDITS

Photographers: Neil Barclay
(pages 39 and 127); Martin
Brigdale (page 161); Nicki Dowey
(pages 9, 11, 13, 17, 21, 23, 25, 27,
29, 41, 67, 69, 77, 81, 93, 97, 101, 115,
119, 121, 125, 135, 139, 141, 145, 147,
149, 153, 155,163, 165, 167 and 169);
Fiona Kennedy (pages 43, 75, 112
and 123); Gareth Morgans
(pages 47, 51, 52, 53, 55 and 111);
Myles New (page 151); Craig
Robertson (pages 15, 18, 19, 31, 34,
35, 36, 45, 60, 61, 64, 65, 78, 79, 85,
87, 99, 105, 107, 109, 113, 137, 143
and 159); Maja Smend (pages 73
and 95); Lucinda Symons (pages
83, 103 and 117); Kate Whitaker
(page 89).

Home Economists:
Anna Burges-Lumsden,
Joanna Farrow, Emma Jane Frost,
Teresa Goldfinch, Alice Hart,
Lucy McKelvie, Kim Morphew,
Aya Nishimura, Katie Rogers,
Bridget Sargeson, Sarah Tildesley,
Kate Trend, Jennifer White and
Mari Mererid Williams.

Stylists:
Susannah Blake, Tamzin
Ferdinando, Wei Tang,
Sarah Tildesley, Helen Trent and
Fanny Ward.

BAKE ME A CAKE
There's always time for cake

EASY PEASY MEALS
Easy meals for every day

LET'S DO BRUNCH
Mouth-watering meals to start your day

CHEAP EATS
Budget-busting ideas that won't break the bank

SALAD DAYS
Oh-so-fresh ideas for fabulous salads

Available online at store.anovabooks.com and from all good bookshops

POSH NOSH
Delicious recipes to impress your guests

PARTY FOOD
Delicious recipes to get the party started

SLOW STOPPERS
Slow-cooked meals packed with flavour

GREAT VEG
Inspired ideas for delicious veggie meals

AL FRESCO EATS
Easy grills, barbecues and picnics

ROAST IT
There's nothing better than a delicious roast

FLASH IN THE PAN
Speed up your meal and stir fry time

GLUTEN-FREE AND EASY
Oh-so-good-for-you recipes that taste great

LOW FAT LOW CAL
Nice recipes don't need to be naughty